# U.S. GAAP AND IFRS: A COMPARATIVE ANALYSIS

## ALLAN B. AFTERMAN
### CPA PH.D.

# THOMSON
## TAX & ACCOUNTING

©2008 Thomson/TTA
395 Hudson Street
New York, NY 10014
ria.thomson.com

ISBN 978-0-7913-6907-4

This publication is designed to provide accurate and authoritative
information in regard to the subject matter covered. It is sold
with the understanding that neither the author nor the publisher is
engaged in rendering legal, accounting, or other professional services. If legal advice or other expert assistance is required, the
services of a competent professional should be sought.

PRINTED IN THE UNITED STATES OF AMERICA

# ¶ 1. Contents

# CONTENTS

# CONTENTS

WG&L

# CONTENTS

# CONTENTS

**WG&L**

# CONTENTS

# Introduction

This publication provides, on a topic-by-topic basis, a comparative analysis of the *main* recognition and measurement requirements of U.S. GAAP and International Financial Reporting Standards (IFRS). By no means does this publication cover all such requirements; and, with the exception of a few topics (e.g., accounting policies, development stage entities, related party transactions, segmental reporting) for which disclosure is the principal element, disclosure requirements are not generally addressed. Moreover, with one exception concerning revenue recognition, no attempt has been made to cover the additional layer of SEC accounting and financial reporting rules and regulations whose application is mandatory for public companies. This publication covers 37 major topics; a discussion of U.S. GAAP appears first under each topic, followed by a discussion of IFRS. The discussions identify the principal authoritative sources for each set of standards. To facilitate comparison, certain major topics are further divided into sub-topics, which are addressed in the same order under the discussions of U.S. GAAP and IFRS. Note that, when either set of standards does not explicitly address a specific topic (or sub-topic), the lack of official guidance is so noted.

### Convergence

In October 2002, the FASB and the International Accounting Standards Board (IASB) entered into a memorandum of understanding (referred to as the Norwalk Agreement) acknowledging their joint commitment to the development of high-quality, compatible accounting standards that could be used for both domestic and cross-border financial reporting. At the Norwalk meeting, both the FASB and IASB pledged to use their best efforts to make their existing financial reporting standards fully compatible as soon as practicable and to coordinate their future work programs to ensure that once achieved, compatibility is maintained.

The two Boards agreed to (1) undertake a short-term project to remove various differences between the two accounting systems that could, with only minor modification, enhance compatibility, (2) remove certain other differences by revising specific existing standards, (3) work jointly on new projects, and (4) encourage their respective interpretive bodies to coordinate their activities.

As part of their short-term convergence effort, the FASB has since amended standards relating to inventory costs, exchanges of productive assets, and accounting changes and error corrections, and the IASB has revised its standards on foreign exchange rates, borrowing costs, and segmental reporting.

It is noteworthy that, as the FASB and the IASB continue to progress toward the convergence of U.S. GAAP and IFRS (but not necessarily toward uniformity or even equivalence), many differences between the two sets of standards remain— even between standards that are broadly similar and that were developed jointly by the two Boards. And, of course, if and when full convergence is achieved, variations in the application of some complicated standards are still likely to exist. Indeed, achieving convergence in practice could prove to be elusive; the European

Committee on Securities Regulation (CESR) notes that the desired level of convergence will have been achieved only when financial statements prepared either under U.S. GAAP or IFRS enable investors to make a similar investment decision.

## A Principles-Based Approach

It is generally accepted that IFRS is a more principles-based set of standards than its U.S. GAAP counterpart. The SEC refers to the IFRS system as "objectives-oriented," which is distinguished from principles-based because, in the SEC Staff's view, a principles-only approach does not provide sufficient implementation guidance to make the standards operational. Nevertheless, both the SEC and the FASB acknowledge that U.S. GAAP is overly rule driven and cumbersome—in part because it comprises so many forms of authoritative pronouncements (i.e., the standards themselves, FASB interpretations and Technical Bulletins, EITF Consensuses, and FASB Staff Positions, and for specific industries, statements of position issued by the American Institute of Certified Public Accountants). In contrast, IFRS consists only of IASB-issued standards and interpretations published by the International Financial Reporting Interpretations Committee (IFRIC). Note, though, that the FASB has embarked on a large-scale codification project that, when completed in 2009, will integrate existing U.S. GAAP (which is estimated to comprise more than 2,000 separate pronouncements covering over 25,000 pages) into a single authoritative retrievable source. In addition, the FASB plans to stop issuing interpretations and technical bulletins but, instead, to provide interpretive guidance and make minor amendments to existing standards through a series of FASB Staff Positions.

## Word-Wide Acceptance of IFRS

The use of IFRS has, over recent years, become increasingly widespread throughout the world. Presently, approximately 100 countries now require or permit the application of IFRS, with other countries having adopted them as their national standards, and with still other countries planning to do so in the near term. All companies whose securities are listed on an EU regulated market that are incorporated in one of the 27 countries comprising the European Union must use IFRS as the basis of preparation for their consolidated statements. In addition, IFRS is required in the three European Economic Area countries of Iceland, Lichtenstein, and Norway, as well as in Australia and New Zealand. Canada and Israel are among the countries planning to adopt IFRS as their national standards in the near future. The IASB expects that by 2011 the number of jurisdictions accepting IFRS, to one degree or another, will exceed 150.

## Potential Use of IFRS by Private Entities

In an attempt to serve the needs of private companies, as well as those with publicly traded securities, the IASB issued an exposure draft of a proposed IFRS for use by small and medium-sized entities (SMEs) having no public accountability. The standard is intended to provide a simplified, self-contained set of accounting and financial reporting principles that are appropriate for smaller, non-listed companies but which are based on concepts included in the full set of IFRS that were developed primarily for listed companies. Essentially, the proposed IFRS reflects three major differences from the full set of IFRS: (1) topics deemed irrelevant to SMEs have been omitted (with cross references to the applicable IFRS, if necessary); (2) only the simplest option among choices in the complete set of IFRS has been included; and (3) various recognition and measurement principles have been simplified.

### Recent SEC Developments

In December 2007, the SEC issued new rules allowing foreign companies to file financial statements that are prepared in conformity with IFRS, without also having to provide reconciliations of reported net income and stockholders' equity to corresponding amounts under U.S. GAAP. The new rules are effective for fiscal years ending on or after November 15, 2007 (i.e., for calendar-year 2008), and apply to any foreign issuer that complies with IFRS either voluntarily or in accordance with the requirements of its home country or the requirements of an exchange on which the issuer's shares are listed. Specifically, the conditions of eligibility are:

- Only IFRS *as issued by the IASB* may be applied.

- The issuer must state unreservedly and explicitly in a note to the financial statements that such statements are in compliance with IFRS as issued by the IASB (and, optionally, may also state that the financial statements are in accordance with its home country standards).

- The issuer's independent auditors must render an opinion concerning compliance with IFRS as issued by the IASB (and, optionally, may also render an opinion regarding compliance with standards required by the issuer's home country).

The new rules also provide temporary transition relief for EU companies that are current SEC registrants that have been preparing their financial statements by applying the so-called carve-out provision of IAS No. 39, *Financial Instruments: Recognition and Measurement* (in respect of hedge accounting for certain instruments), as permitted by the European Union (but that otherwise comply with IFRS as issued by the IASB). Under such relief, the SEC will accept financial statements without reconciliations to U.S. GAAP for each of the first two financial years (and *only* for such years) ending after November 15, 2007, provided that the issuer also includes an audited *reconciliation to IFRS* as issued by the IASB.

In August 2007, the SEC published a Concept Release seeking information about the public's interest in permitting *U.S. domestic registrants* to prepare their financial statements in accordance with IFRS. The Commission advises that the move to allow U.S. public companies the option to choose IFRS instead of U.S. GAAP as the basis of preparation of financial statements furnished to investors and filed with the SEC would be a complex endeavor. The SEC has identified the following matters that could pose difficulties in permitting such a choice:

- Education and training. The use of IFRS by U.S. issuers would create the need for effective training and education among financial statement preparers, auditors, analysts, and other users.

- Application in practice. The Commission's experience in assessing the proper application of IFRS by U.S. issuers would, at least initially, be limited to its experience in evaluating IFRS application by foreign companies.
- The absence of IASB standards. At the present time, only limited IFRS guidance exists in respect of accounting for insurance contracts and extractive activities; in addition, specific guidance is lacking concerning the accounting treatment for (1) common control mergers, (2) recapitalizations, (3) reorganizations, and (4) acquisitions of minority interests.
- Auditing. Accounting firms (particularly the smaller ones) would have to determine whether it is economically feasible to make the initial and ongoing investments in quality control systems to ensure that audits of IFRS financial statements are competently delivered and adequately supervised.
- Differing views of regulators. Despite mechanisms now in place, it is possible that a securities regulator (whether the SEC or its counterpart in another country) would have to state a view on an accounting issue that has caused significant practice difficulties but which has not been addressed by the IASB or IFRIC, and such view could be different from those of securities regulators in other jurisdictions.
- Integration with existing regulations. Various articles of Regulation S-X contain a substantial degree of detail in respect of the form and content of financial statements, whereas IFRS does not provide specific conventions regarding the form or content of the income statement; in addition, various Regulation S-K items contain disclosure requirements that refer to specific U.S. GAAP pronouncements. If U.S. issuers are allowed to prepare IFRS financial statements, the Commission would have to adopt policies regarding the applicability of certain Regulation S-X and Regulation S-K requirements to such issuers that could differ from those applicable to other U.S. companies using U.S. GAAP.

Such obstacles notwithstanding, the SEC points out at least two strong market forces that could provide an impetus in the future for U.S. issuers to request the Commission's acceptance of IFRS:

- As the number of jurisdictions requiring or allowing the use of IFRS grows (and thus as more non-U.S. companies report their financial results in accordance with IFRS), there may be pressure on U.S. issuers in a particular industry, sector, or market to prepare financial reports on the basis of IFRS to enable more efficient comparisons among companies.
- As more countries accept IFRS financial statements for local regulatory or statutory filing purposes, subsidiaries of U.S. companies based in those jurisdictions will be preparing and filing their local financial statements using IFRS.

The SEC acknowledges that U.S. companies without significant customers or operations outside the United States (which group is more likely to comprise smaller public companies) may not have the market incentives to prepare financial statements using IFRS. Moreover, if the Commission were to permit U.S. companies to file IFRS financial statements, investors and other market participants would be forced to understand and work with *both* IFRS and U.S. GAAP (because not all U.S. public companies would be likely to choose to prepare IFRS statements). Also, as practical matters (1) U.S. issuers may have loan agreements and other contracts that include U.S. GAAP-based covenants, and (2) U.S. companies are likely to use their U.S. GAAP-prepared financial statements as the basis for filings with regulators and local taxing authorities that require U.S. GAAP information.

# ¶ 100. The Basic Financial Statements—Form and Content
U.S. GAAP

## ¶ 101. Main Authoritative Sources

- ARB No. 43, *Restatement and Revision of Accounting Research Bulletins* (Chapter 2A, "Comparative Financial Statements")
- ARB No. 43, *Restatement and Revision of Accounting Research Bulletins* (Chapter 3A, "Current Assets and Current Liabilities")
- ARB No. 43, *Restatement and Revision of Accounting Research Bulletins* (Chapter 3B, "Offsetting Securities against Taxes Payable")
- APB Opinion No. 12, *Omnibus Opinion—1967*
- SFAS No. 6, *Classification of Short-Term Obligations Expected to Be Refinanced*
- SFAS No. 95, *Statement of Cash Flows*
- SFAS No. 130, *Reporting Comprehensive Income*
- FASB Interpretation No. 39, *Offsetting of Amounts Related to Certain Contracts*

## ¶ 102. Comparative Statements

It is ordinarily desirable that the balance sheet, the income statement, the statement of retained earnings (and/or the statement of stockholders' equity and, if presented separately, the statement of accumulated comprehensive income), and the statement of cash flows be given for one or more preceding years as well as for the current year. Notes to the financial statements of preceding years presented for comparative purposes should be repeated to the extent that they continue to be of significance.

## ¶ 103. Current Assets

Current assets comprise cash and other assets or resources commonly identified as those that are reasonably expected to be realized in cash or sold, or consumed during the normal operating cycle of the business. Prepaid expenses are not current assets in the sense that they will be converted into cash but, rather, in the sense that, if not paid in advance, they would require the use of current assets during the operating cycle. Normally, a one-year time period should be used as a basis for the classification of current assets; when, however, the entity's operating cycle is more than 12 months, it should be used. If an entity has no clearly defined operating cycle, the one-year rule should govern for classification of current assets.

## ¶ 104. Current Liabilities

The term current liabilities is used principally to designate obligations whose liquidation is reasonably expected to require the use of existing resources properly classifiable as current assets, or the creation of other current liabilities. A short-term obligation intended to be refinanced on a long-term basis may be included in noncurrent liabilities if the company can support its intention with an ability to accomplish the refinancing. Evidence of that ability may be demonstrated as follows:

- The company refinances the short-term debt after the balance sheet but before the financial statements are issued.

- Before the financial statements are issued, the company enters into an agreement that clearly permits the refinancing on terms that are readily determinable, and (1) the agreement does not expire within one year from the balance-sheet date and is not cancelable or callable by the lender, (2) no violation of any provision in the financing agreement exists at the balance-sheet date, or after that date but before the statements are issued (or if one does exist, a waiver has not been obtained), and (3) the lender is expected to be financially capable of honoring the agreement.

In respect of obligations that are callable by the creditor, the following must be classified as current liabilities:

- Obligations due on demand or that will be due on demand within one year (or operating cycle, if longer) from the date of the financial statements, even though payment may not be expected to be made within that period.

- Long-term obligations that are or will be callable by the creditor because either the debtor has violated a provision of the debt agreement or, if the violation is not cured within a specified grace period, the obligation will be callable.

If, at the date of the financial statements, the debtor is in violation of a covenant of a debt agreement, the related debt must be considered current unless one of the following conditions is met:

- The creditor has waived or subsequently lost the right to demand repayment for more than one year (or operating cycle, if longer) from the date of the financial statement.

- It is probable that the debtor will cure the violation within a specified grace period, thus preventing the debt from being callable.

## ¶ 105. Valuation Allowances

Accumulated allowances for depreciation and depletion and asset valuation allowances should be deducted from the assets or groups of assets to which they relate.

## ¶ 106. Offsetting

Offsetting of assets and liabilities in the balance sheet is improper except when a right of setoff exists. Accordingly, the offset of cash or other assets against a tax liability or other amounts owing to governmental bodies is not acceptable except when it is clear that a purchase of securities (that are acceptable for the payment of taxes) is in substance an advance payment of taxes that will be payable in the relatively near future (i.e., such that the purchase is tantamount to the prepayment of taxes).

In general, offsetting of assets and liabilities is inappropriate unless all of the following conditions are met:

- Each of two parties owes the other determinable amounts.
- The reporting party has the right to set off the amount owed to the other party with the amount owed by the other party.
- The reporting party intends to set off the amounts.
- The right of setoff is enforceable by law.

Taken together, if all of these conditions are satisfied, the "right of setoff" exists.

In addition, offsetting is permitted of (1) fair value amounts for derivative instruments executed with the same counterparty under a master netting arrangement (even absent the condition relating to the reporting entity's intention to set off), and (2) recognized fair value amounts representing the right to reclaim cash collateral or the obligation to return such collateral against recognized fair values for derivatives under the same conditions (i.e., that are executed with the same counterparty under the same master netting arrangement). A master netting arrangement exists if the reporting entity has multiple contracts (whether for the same type or different types of derivative instruments), with a single counterparty that are subject to a contractual agreement that provides for the net settlement of all contracts through a single payment in a single currency in the event of default on or termination of any one contract.

## ¶ 107. Cash Flow Statement

Cash includes equivalents, which are defined as short-term, highly liquid investments that are both readily convertible into cash and so close to maturity that the risk of changes in value because of interest-rate fluctuations is insignificant. In general, only investments with *original* maturities of three months or less qualify as cash equivalents.

Cash inflows and outflows should be classified by operating, investing, or financing activities. If a cash receipt or payment has characteristics of more than one type of activity, its classification is dependent on the predominant source of cash flow for the item. Interest and dividend income must, however, be classified as cash inflows from operating activities, and interest expense and income tax expense must be classified as cash outflows from operating activities. Cash flows resulting from futures contracts, option contracts, or swap contracts that are accounted for as hedges of identifiable transactions or events may be classified in the same category as the cash flows from the item being hedged.

Cash flows from operating activities may be presented either on the direct or indirect method. Under the direct method, major classes of gross cash receipts and gross cash payments are presented. If the direct method is applied, the following classes of operating receipts and payments are required:

- Cash collected from customers.

- Interest and dividends received.
- Other operating receipts.
- Cash paid to employees and other suppliers of goods or services.
- Interest paid.
- Income taxes paid.
- Other operating payments.

If the direct method is used, a separate reconciliation of net income to cash flow from operating activities must also be presented.

In general, cash inflows and outflows must be reported separately (i.e., the right of offset within or among categories of activities does not exist). For certain items, however, for which the turnover is quick, the amounts are large, and the maturities are short (e.g., demand deposits of a bank and customer accounts payable of a broker-dealer), net changes may be reported on the statement of cash flows.

Information about all investing and financing activities must be disclosed. Disclosure of such activities that do not affect cash may be presented in narrative form or summarized in a schedule. If a transaction is part cash and part non-cash, the cash portion should be reported in the statement of cash flows and the non-cash portion should be reported in narrative form or in a schedule summarizing non-cash investing and financing activities.

A company with foreign currency transactions or foreign operations should show the reporting currency equivalent of foreign currency cash flows using exchange rates in effect at the time of the cash flow. The effect of exchange-rate changes on cash balances held in foreign currencies should be reported separately within the body of the statement of cash flows as part of the change in cash and cash equivalents for the period.

## ¶ 108. Comprehensive Income

The term comprehensive income is defined as:

- The change in equity (net assets) of a business enterprise during a period from transactions and other events and circumstances from non-owner sources. It includes all changes in equity during a period except those resulting from investments by owners and distributions to owners.

Comprehensive income (and its components) may be presented in any of the following financial statements:

- In a separate statement of comprehensive income (which must begin with net income).
- In a statement of changes in equity.
- Below the total of net income or loss in the income statement.

Accumulated other comprehensive income should be reported in the equity section of the balance sheet separately from all other equity elements. In addition, the aggregate balance in each component of accumulated other comprehensive income must be shown on the balance sheet itself, in a statement of change in equity, or in a note to the financial statements. Specific components of other comprehensive income for a period may be displayed either net of related tax effects or before tax effects (with a single amount for the aggregate tax impact of all items of other comprehensive income).

Only the following components comprise other comprehensive income:

- Foreign currency translation adjustments.

- Gains and losses on foreign currency transactions designated and effective as hedges of a net investment in a foreign entity.

- Gains and losses on intercompany foreign currency transactions that are of a long-term nature when the entities to the transactions are consolidated, combined, or accounted for by the equity method.

- Gains or losses, prior service costs or credits, and transition assets or obligations associated with pension or other postretirement benefits.

- Unrealized gains or losses on available-for-sale securities.

- Subsequent temporary changes in the fair value of available-for-sale securities previously written down as impaired.

Reclassification adjustments may be required in order to avoid double counting of items that are included in net income for a given period but which have also been considered part of other comprehensive income in an earlier period. Reclassification adjustments may be shown either in the statement in which other comprehensive income is reported or in a note to the financial statements. Display may be either gross or net, except for minimum pension liability adjustments, which must be displayed on a net basis.

IFRS

# ¶ 109. Main Authoritative Sources

- IAS No. 1, *Presentation of Financial Statements*
- IAS No. 7, *Cash Flow Statements*
- IAS No. 12, *Income Taxes*
- IAS No. 32, *Financial Instruments: Disclosure and Presentation*

# ¶ 110. Comparative Statements

Financial statements should be presented at least annually. Comparative information should be disclosed in respect of the previous period for all amounts reported in the financial statements (i.e., comparative statements for the previous period, at a minimum, are required). In addition, comparative narrative information (e.g., in notes to the financial statements) should be included when it is relevant to an understanding of the current period's statements.

## ¶ 111. Current Assets

An asset should be classified as current when it satisfies any of the following criteria:

- It is expected to be realized in or is intended for sale or consumption in the entity's normal operating cycle.
- It is held primarily for the purpose of being traded.
- It is expected to be realized within 12 months after the balance sheet date.
- It is cash or a cash equivalent, unless it is restricted from being exchanged or used to settle a liability for at least 12 months after the balance sheet date.

An entity's operating cycle is the time between the acquisition of assets for processing and their realization in cash or cash equivalents. When the entity's normal operating cycle is not clearly identifiable, its duration is assumed to be 12 months. Note that deferred tax assets may *not* be classified as current.

## ¶ 112. Current Liabilities

A liability should be classified as current when it satisfies any of the following conditions:

- It is expected to be settled in the entity's normal operating cycle.
- It is held primarily for the purpose of being traded.
- It is due to be settled within 12 months after the balance sheet date.
- The entity does not have an unconditional right to defer settlement of the liability for at least 12 months after the balance sheet date.

Note, however, that deferred tax liabilities may *not* be classified as current.

If an entity expects (and has the discretion) to refinance or roll over an obligation for at least 12 months after the balance sheet date under an existing loan facility, the obligation should be classified as non-current (even if it would otherwise be due within a shorter period). When, however, refinancing or rolling over the obligation is not at the discretion of the entity (e.g., there is no agreement to refinance in place), the obligation should be classified as a current liability.

When an entity breaches an undertaking under a long-term loan agreement on or before the balance sheet date (and thus the liability becomes payable on demand), it should be classified as current, even if the lender has agreed, after the balance sheet date and before authorization of the financial statements for issuance, not to demand payment as a consequence of the breach. The liability should be classified as non-current, however, if the lender has agreed by the balance sheet date to provide a period of grace ending at least 12 months after the balance sheet date, within which the entity can rectify the breach and during which the lender cannot demand immediate repayment.

## ¶ 113. Valuation Allowances

IFRS does not directly address the general use of asset valuation allowances, except that the proper use of such allowances (in accordance with specific standards) does not violate the overall prohibition of offsetting.

## ¶ 114. Offsetting

Assets and liabilities, and income and expenses, should not be offset, unless required or permitted by a standard or an interpretation. In the course of ordinary activities, however, other transactions are undertaken that do not generate revenue but are incidental to the entity's main revenue-generating activities. The results of such transactions may be presented, by netting income with expenses arising on the same transaction, when such presentation reflects the substance of the transaction or other event, by netting any income with related expenses arising on the same transaction. In addition, gains and losses arising from a group of similar transactions may be reported on a net basis (e.g., foreign exchange gains and losses or gains and losses arising on financial instruments held for trading). Such gains and losses should, however, be reported separately if they are material.

Current tax assets and current tax liabilities may be offset if the entity:

- Has a legally enforceable right of offset.
- Intends either to settle on a net basis or to realize the asset and settle the liability simultaneously.

Deferred tax assets and deferred tax liabilities may be offset if:

- The entity has a legally enforceable right to set off current tax assets against current tax liabilities.
- The deferred tax assets and the deferred tax liabilities relate to income taxes levied by the same taxation authority on either (1) the same taxable entity, or (2) different taxable entities that intend either to settle current tax liabilities and assets on a net basis or to realize the assets and settle the liabilities simultaneously in each future period in which significant amounts of deferred tax liabilities or assets are expected to be settled or recovered.

A financial asset and a financial liability should be offset only when an entity:

- Has a legally enforceable right of offset.
- Intends either to settle on a net basis or to realize the asset and settle the liability simultaneously.

In respect of a financial asset that does not qualify for derecognition, the transferred asset should not be offset against the associated liability.

## ¶ 115. Cash Flow Statement

Cash comprises cash on hand and demand deposits. Cash equivalents are short-term, highly liquid investments that are readily convertible to known amounts of cash and that are subject to an insignificant risk of changes in value. Normally an investment qualifies as a cash equivalent if it has a short maturity of three months or less from the date of acquisition.

Cash flows should be classified by operating, investing and financing activities. Cash flows from interest and dividends received and paid should each be disclosed separately and classified in a consistent manner from period to period as either operating, investing or financing activities. Dividends paid may be classified as a financing cash flow or as a component of cash flows from operating activities. Income tax cash flows should be classified as cash flows from operating activities, unless they can be specifically identified with financing or investing activities.

Cash flows from operating activities may be reported on either the direct or indirect method. Under the direct method, major classes of gross cash receipts and gross cash payments are disclosed; under the indirect method, profit or loss is adjusted for the effects of non-cash transactions.

Generally, major classes of cash flows should be reported on a gross basis. Net presentation is permitted, however, for the following:

- Cash receipts and payments on behalf of customers when the cash flows reflect the activities of the customer rather than those of the entity.
- Cash receipts and payments for items in which the turnover is quick, the amounts are large, and the maturities are short.

Investing and financing transactions that do not require the use of cash or cash equivalents should be excluded from the cash flow statement. Such transactions should, however, be disclosed in a way that provides all the relevant information about investing and financing activities.

Unrealized gains and losses arising from changes in foreign currency exchange rates are not cash flows; the effect of exchange rate changes on cash and cash equivalents held or due in a foreign currency should, however, be reported separately from cash flows from operating, investing, and financing activities and should include the differences, if any, had those cash flows been reported at end-of-period exchange rates.

## ¶ 116. Comprehensive Income

**Note:** The following discussion is based on revised IAS No. 1, which becomes effective from January 1, 2009, with earlier application permitted. Under prior IAS No. 1, the term "comprehensive income" is not addressed; however, the statement of changes in equity (or the statement of recognized income and expense) requires disclosure of (1) profit or loss for the period, and (2) each item of income and expense for the period that, pursuant to other IFRS, has been recognized directly in equity, and (3) total income and expense for the period.

Other comprehensive income comprises items of income and expense that are not recognized in profit or loss as required or permitted by other IFRS. The components of other comprehensive income include:

- Changes in revaluation surplus.

- Actuarial gains and losses on defined benefit plans.
- Gains and losses arising from translating the financial statements of a foreign operation.
- Gains and losses on remeasuring available-for-sale financial assets.
- The effective portion of gains and losses on hedging instruments.

Total comprehensive income represents the change in equity during a period resulting from transactions and other events, other than changes resulting from transactions with owners in their capacity as owners.

Total comprehensive income comprises all components of profit or loss and other comprehensive income.

All items of income and expense recognized in a period may be presented either:

- In a single statement of comprehensive income.
- In a separate income statement that displays the components of profit or loss and in a separate statement of comprehensive income that displays the components of other comprehensive income.

Components of other comprehensive income may be presented either net of related tax effects or before related tax effects together with the aggregate amount of income tax relating to all components.

Reclassification adjustments, which represent amounts reclassified to profit or loss in the current period that were recognized in other comprehensive income in the current or previous periods, should be disclosed either in the statement of comprehensive income or in notes to the financial statements. Display of reclassification adjustments may be on a gross or net basis.

# ¶ 200. First-Time Adoption

U.S. GAAP

## ¶ 201. Main Authoritative Sources

- None - not directly addressed

Unlike IFRS, there is no specific pronouncement covering the first-time adoption of U.S. GAAP (in the context of having switched from the accounting standards of another jurisdiction); first-time adoption, however, requires that the current year's financial statements (and those of prior years presented for comparative purposes) be in full compliance with U.S. standards.

IFRS

## ¶ 202. Main Authoritative Sources

- IFRS 1, *First-Time Adoption of International Financial Reporting Standards*

An opening IFRS balance sheet should be prepared as of the date of transition to IFRS, which represents the starting point for an entity's accounting under IFRS. In the opening IFRS balance sheet, the entity must (1) recognize all assets and liabilities whose recognition is required by IFRS, (2) not recognize items as assets or liabilities if IFRS does not permit such recognition, (3) reclassify items that it recognized under previous GAAP as one type of asset, liability or component of equity, but are a different type of asset, liability or component of equity under IFRS, and (4) apply IFRS in measuring all recognized assets and liabilities. Adjustments resulting from the foregoing procedures should be recognized directly in retained earnings at the date of transition.

An entity should use the same accounting policies in its opening IFRS balance sheet and throughout all periods presented in its first IFRS financial statements. Generally, such policies must comply with each IFRS effective at the reporting date for its first set of IFRS financial statements.

The following major exceptions apply, however, to the general rule that the opening IFRS balance sheet must comply with each IFRS in force at the transition date:

- Business combinations occurring prior to transition *may* continue to be accounted for as they were under previous national GAAP.

- An item of property, plant, and equipment *may* be measured at fair value at the date of transition and designate such fair value as deemed cost.

- All previously unrecognized actuarial gains and losses relating to employee benefit plans *may* be recognized at the date of transition.

- The cumulative translation adjustment existing at the date of transition not previously classified as a component of stockholders' equity *may* be deemed to have a zero value.

- If the liability portion of a previously issued compound financial instrument is no longer outstanding at the date of transition, the remaining portion *need not* be split between retained earnings and paid-in capital.
- A financial instrument *may* be designated a financial asset or liability at fair value through profit and loss or as available for sale at the date of transition.
- IFRS 2, *Share-Based Payment, need not* be applied to (1) equity instruments granted before November 7, 2002, or (2) liabilities settled before January 2005.
- A previously designated hedging relationship not qualifying for hedge accounting under IFRS 39, *Financial Instruments: Recognition and Measurement, must* not be reflected in the opening IFRS balance sheet.
- Estimates made under IFRS at the date of transition *must* be consistent with estimates made for the same date under previous GAAP (after adjustments to reflect any difference in accounting policies), unless there is objective evidence that those estimates were in error.

An entity's first set of IFRS financial statements should include at least one year of comparative IFRS information. An explanation should be provided regarding the manner in which the transition from previous GAAP to IFRS affected reported financial position, financial performance, and cash flows.

In addition:

- Reconciliations should be presented of reported equity under previous GAAP to equity under IFRS as of (1) the date of transition to IFRS, and (2) the end of the latest period presented in the most recent annual financial statements under previous GAAP.
- A reconciliation should be provided of the profit or loss reported under previous GAAP for the latest period in the most recent annual financial statements to profit or loss under IFRS for the same period.

The first set of IFRS financial statements must contain an explicit and unreserved statement of compliance with IFRS.

# ¶ 300. Financial Assets and Financial Liabilities

## U.S. GAAP

## ¶ 301. Main Authoritative Sources

- APB Opinion No. 12, *Omnibus Opinion—1967*
- APB Opinion No. 21, *Interest on Receivables and Payables*
- APB Opinion No. 26, *Early Extinguishment of Debt*
- SFAS No. 15, *Accounting by Debtors and Creditors for Troubled Debt Restructurings*
- SFAS No. 114, *Accounting by Creditors for Impairment of a Loan*
- SFAS No. 115, *Accounting for Certain Debt and Equity Securities*
- SFAS No. 140, *Accounting for Transfers and Servicing of Financial Assets and Extinguishments of Liabilities*
- SFAS No. 150, *Accounting for Certain Financial Instruments with Characteristics of Both Debt and Equity*
- SFAS No. 159, *The Fair Value Option for Financial Assets and Financial Liabilities*

## ¶ 302. Marketable Securities

At acquisition and at each subsequent reporting date, equity securities having readily determinable fair values and all debt securities should be classified into one of the following three reporting categories:

- Held-to-maturity securities.
- Trading securities.
- Available-for-sale securities

The fair value of an equity security is readily determinable if the sales price or bid-and-asked quotations are currently available on a securities exchange registered with the SEC or in the over-the-counter market, provided that such prices or quotations for the over-the-counter market are publicly reported by the National Association of Securities Dealers Automated Quotations systems or in the so-called pink sheets. For debt securities that have no quoted market price, that trade only in principal-to-principal markets, or that do not trade regularly, fair value should be estimated using one or more of the following techniques, among others that may be appropriate:

- Discounted cash flow analysis.
- Fundamental analysis.
- Matrix pricing.
- Option-adjusted spread models.

Equity securities for which fair values are not readily determinable should be carried at cost, or, if applicable, on the equity method.

Only debt securities should be classified as held to maturity and only if the entity has both the positive intent and the ability to hold those securities to maturity.

Debt securities should not be classified as held to maturity if they might be sold in response to one or more of the following factors:

- Changes in market interest rates.
- Changes in prepayment risk.
- Liquidity requirements.
- Changes in the availability of and the yield on alternative investments.
- Changes in funding sources and terms.
- Changes in foreign currency risk.

The following changes in circumstances, however, may cause an entity to modify its intention to hold a given security to maturity without raising doubt about its intent to hold other debt securities to maturity in the future:

- Evidence of a significant deterioration in the issuer's creditworthiness.
- A change in tax law that eliminates or reduces the tax-exempt status of interest on the debt security.
- A major business combination or major disposition of a component of the entity that necessitates the sale or transfer of held-to-maturity securities to maintain the enterprise's existing interest rate risk position or credit risk policy.
- A change in statutory or regulatory requirements significantly modifying either what constitutes a permissible investment or the maximum level of investments in certain kinds of securities, thereby causing an enterprise to dispose of a held-to-maturity security.
- A significant increase in the industry's capital requirements by the regulator that causes the enterprise to downsize by selling held-to-maturity securities.
- A significant increase in the risk weights of debt securities used for regulatory risk-based capital purposes.

If a sale or transfer of a held-to-maturity security is made for a reason other than for any of the aforementioned reasons, any remaining held-to-maturity securities should be reclassified to the available-for-sale category when the sale or transfer represents a material contradiction to the entity's stated intent to hold those securities until maturity or when a pattern of such sales has occurred. Held-to-maturity securities should be carried at amortized cost.

Debt securities not held to maturity and equity securities that have readily determinable fair values should be classified as trading securities if they:

- Are held for short periods of time
- Have been acquired with the expectation of a profit from short-term price differences.

Trading securities should be carried at fair value, with unrealized holding gains and losses accounted for in current earnings. Held-to-maturity securities should be carried at amortized cost. Debt securities and equity securities having readily determinable fair values that are not otherwise classified should be categorized as securities held for sale and carried at fair value, with unrealized holding gains and losses reported as other comprehensive income.

The transfer of a security between categories should be accounted for at fair value. Unrealized holding gains and losses should be accounted for as follows:

- For a security transferred from the trading category, the unrealized gain or loss at the date of transfer will already have been recognized in income and should not be reversed.

- For a security transferred to the trading category, the unrealized holding gain or loss will not yet have been recognized and should be reflected in current earnings.

- For a debt security transferred to the available-for-sale category from the held-to-maturity category, the unrealized holding gain or loss should be recognized in other comprehensive income.

- For a debt security transferred to the held-to-maturity category from the available-for-sale category, the unrealized holding gain or loss should remain in accumulated other comprehensive income but should be amortized over the remaining term of the security.

An investment in either held-to-maturity or available-for-sale securities is deemed impaired if its fair value is less than its cost. If impairment is considered other than temporary, an impairment loss should be recognized as the difference between the investment's cost and its fair value as of the end of the reporting period (and should not take into account any partial recovery of the fair value deficiency subsequent to the balance sheet date). After recognition of the impairment loss, the fair value to which the investment has been written down becomes its new cost basis (which should not be upwardly adjusted for subsequent partial or complete recovery of the fair value deficiency). In respect of available-for-sale securities whose impairment is judged to be only temporary, subsequent increases in fair value (and further subsequent temporary decreases) should be included in other comprehensive income.

## ¶ 303. Other Financial Assets

When a note receivable is exchanged for property, goods, or services in an arm's-length transaction, the presumption is that the stipulated rate of interest is fair. If there is no stated rate or an unreasonable rate or the face amount of the note differs materially from the cash sales price of the property, goods, or services, then the exchange is valued at either (1) the fair value of the property, goods, or services or (2) an amount that reasonably approximates the market value of the note, whichever is more clearly determinable. In the absence of either of these amounts, the present value of the note is determined by discounting future payments using an imputed rate that approximates the rate that an independent borrower and lender would have negotiated in a similar transaction. Any difference between the face amount of the note and its present value is accounted for as a discount and amortized over the life of the note by the interest method or any other method that produces approximately the same results.

A transfer of all or a portion of financial assets should be accounted for as a sale (but only to the extent that consideration other than beneficial interests in the transferred assets is received), provided that the transferor surrenders control over the assets. Surrender of control is deemed to have occurred only if all of the following conditions have been met:

- The transferred assets have been isolated from the transferor (and any of its consolidated affiliates). The transferred assets must be put presumptively beyond the reach of the transferor and its creditors even in the transferor's bankruptcy or other form of receivership.

- Each transferee has the right to pledge or exchange the assets received and no condition (1) constrains the transferee from taking advantage of that right, and (2) provides more than a trivial benefit to the transferor.

- The transferor does not maintain effective control over the transferred assets by way of an agreement that both entitles and obligates the transferor to repurchase or redeem the assets before maturity or by means of its unilateral ability to cause the holder to return specific assets.

Transfers that do not meet all of the foregoing criteria may not be accounted for as sales; rather, they should be treated as secured borrowings.

Upon completion of a transfer of financial assets satisfying the conditions for sale accounting, the transferor-seller should:

- Derecognize all assets sold.

- Recognize all assets obtained and liabilities incurred in consideration as proceeds from the sale.

- Initially measure assets obtained at fair value; if it is not practicable to do so, such assets should be recorded at a zero value.

- Initially measure liabilities assumed (including the recourse obligations) at fair value; if it is not practicable to do so, no gain should be recognized on the transaction and such liabilities should be recorded at the greater of (1) any excess of the fair values of assets obtained less the fair values of other liabilities assumed or incurred over the sum of the carrying values of the assets transferred, or (2) a reasonable estimate of the amounts of such liabilities.

- Immediately recognize any gain or loss on the sale.

## ¶ 304. Financial Liabilities

A liability is deemed extinguished if either of the following conditions is met:

- The debtor pays the creditor and is thus relieved of its obligation. Payment may be in the form of cash, other financial assets, goods, or services; payment also includes reacquisition by the debtor of its outstanding debt securities.

- The debtor is legally released from being the primary obligor, either judicially or by the creditor.

If debt is extinguished prior to its scheduled maturity (early extinguishment), a gain or loss may arise on the transaction equal to the difference between the carrying value of the debt and the amount of consideration paid to extinguish the liability.

## ¶ 305. Financial Instruments with Characteristics of Both Debt and Equity

Freestanding financial instruments (i.e., those entered into separately from an entity's other financial instruments or equity transactions or that are legally detachable and separately exercisable) having characteristics of both liabilities and equity must be classified as liabilities.

A mandatorily redeemable financial instrument should be classified as a liability if it requires the issuer to redeem the instrument by transferring assets at specified or determinable dates upon an event certain to occur, unless redemption is mandatory only upon the liquidation or termination of the entity. Such freestanding financial instruments should be shown as liabilities in the balance sheet (i.e., they may not be positioned between liabilities and stockholders' equity). A financial instrument that contains a conditional obligation to redeem the instrument upon an event that is not certain to occur becomes mandatorily redeemable when (1) the condition is resolved, or (2) the event actually happens or becomes certain to happen. Hence, such an instrument must be assessed at each reporting date to determine whether the triggering event is no longer conditional.

In general, mandatorily redeemable financial instruments should be measured initially at fair value, with subsequent changes in fair value recognized in current earnings.

## ¶ 306. The Fair Value Option

Under the fair value option, entities are permitted, at specified election dates, to measure eligible items at fair value. Unrealized gains and losses on eligible items measured at fair value must be reported in current earnings.

Generally, the fair value option may be applied to (1) a recognized financial asset or financial liability, or (2) a firm commitment that would otherwise not be recognized at inception that involves only financial instruments. The fair value option may be chosen for an individual eligible item without electing it for other identical items.

The decision to elect the fair value option may be made only on the date on which one of the following occurs:

- Initial recognition of the item or entry into an eligible firm commitment.

- An event takes place requiring an eligible item to be measured at fair value at the time of the event but does not require fair value measurement on an ongoing basis.

## ¶ 307. Troubled Debt Restructurings

The accounting by creditors depends on the type of restructuring. There are essentially three types of arrangements:

- Receipt of assets in full satisfaction.
- Modification of terms.
- Receipt of assets in partial settlement together with modification of terms.

A creditor that receives from a debtor in full satisfaction of a receivable either (1) receivables from third parties, real estate, or other assets, or both, or (2) shares of stock or other evidence of an equity interest in the debtor, or both, should account for those assets (including an equity interest) at their fair value at the time of the restructuring. A creditor that receives long-lived assets from a debtor that will be sold in full satisfaction of a receivable should account for those assets at their fair value less cost to sell. The excess of (1) the recorded investment in the receivable satisfied over (2) the fair value of assets received (less cost to sell, if applicable) should be recognized as a loss. After a troubled debt restructuring, a creditor should account for assets received in satisfaction of a receivable in the same manner as if the assets had been acquired for cash.

If the arrangement calls only for a modification of terms, the creditor should account for the effects of the restructuring as a loan impairment. In general, a loan is impaired when it is probable that the creditor will not be able to collect principal and interest in accordance with the terms of the agreement. In measuring impairment, the creditor may use (1) the present value of future cash flows, (2) observable market prices, if available, or (3) the fair value of collateral, if the receivable is so-called collateral dependent (i.e., repayment is expected solely from the underlying collateral).

If the restructuring involves both the receipt of assets and a modification of terms, the recorded investment in the receivable first is reduced by the fair value of assets received. Then the remaining receivable is compared with the present value of future cash flows (or observable market prices or the fair value of collateral) to determine whether it is impaired.

If the debtor transfers assets or grants an equity interest in full satisfaction of the debt, a gain should be recognized by the debtor in the amount of any excess of the carrying amount of the debt over the fair value of the assets (or equity interest) transferred.

If the arrangement calls only for a modification of terms, the debtor should account for the effects of the restructuring prospectively and should not change the carrying amount of the debt at the time of restructuring unless the carrying amount exceeds the total future cash payments specified by the new terms. Interest expense should be computed by the interest method; the new effective rate will be the discount rate that equates the present value of the future cash payments with the carrying amount of the debt.

If, however, the total future cash payments specified by the new terms, including both payments designated as interest and those designated as principal, are less than the carrying amount of the debt, the debtor should (1) reduce the carrying amount to an amount equal to the total future cash payments specified by the new terms, and (2) recognize a gain on restructuring equal to the amount of the reduction. Thereafter, all cash payments under the terms should be accounted for as reductions of the carrying amount of the debt, and no interest expense is to be recognized for any period between the restructuring and maturity of the debt.

If the arrangement involves partial settlement of the debt by transferring assets or granting an equity interest (or both) to the creditor and by modification of the terms of the remaining payable, the assets transferred or an equity interest granted in that partial settlement should be measured in accordance with the accounting for assets (or equity interest) transferred in full settlement, and the carrying amount of the debt should be reduced by the total fair value of those assets or equity interest. Any difference between the fair value and the carrying amount of assets transferred to the creditor should be recognized as a gain or loss on transfer of assets. No gain should be recognized unless the remaining carrying amount of the debt exceeds the total future cash payments specified by the terms of the debt remaining unsettled after the restructuring.

IFRS

## ¶ 308. Main Authoritative Sources

- IAS 32, *Financial Instruments: Disclosure and Presentation*
- IAS 39, *Financial Instruments: Recognition and Measurement*

## ¶ 309. Financial Assets

Financial assets fall into one of the following categories:

- Held-to-maturity.
- Fair value through profit or loss.
- Available-for-sale.
- Loans and receivables.

Held-to-maturity investments are non-derivative financial assets with fixed or determinable payments and fixed maturities that an entity has the positive intention and ability to hold to maturity. A financial asset at fair value through profit or loss is one that is acquired for the purpose of selling it in the near term or part of a portfolio of identified financial instruments that are managed together and for which there is evidence of a recent actual pattern of short-term profit-taking. Available-for-sale financial assets are those that are designated as available for sale or are not included in another category. Loans and receivables are financial assets (1) with fixed or determinable payments, (2) that are not quoted in an active market, (3) do not qualify as trading assets, and (4) have not been designated as fair value through profit or loss or as available for sale.

Financial assets may not be classified as held to maturity if the entity has, during the current year or during the two preceding years (i.e., the so-called tainting period), sold or reclassified more than an insignificant amount of held-to-maturity investments before maturity other than sales or reclassifications that:

- Are so close to maturity or the financial asset's call date (e.g., less than three months before maturity) that changes in the market rate of interest would not have a significant effect on the financial asset's fair value.

- Occur after collection of substantially all of the financial asset's original principal through scheduled payments or prepayments.

- Are attributable to an isolated event that is beyond the entity's control, is non-recurring and could not have been reasonably anticipated.

Note that, if sales or reclassifications of more than an insignificant amount of held-to-maturity investments do not meet any of the foregoing conditions, any remaining held-to-maturity investments must be reclassified as available for sale.

Upon initial recognition, a financial asset should be measured at fair value. Subsequently, loans and receivables and held-to-maturity financial assets should be measured at amortized cost. Financial assets at fair value through profit or loss should subsequently be measured, and available-for-sale assets should be measured at fair value. Gains or losses from changes in fair values should be recognized in (1) profit or loss for financial assets carried at fair value through profit or loss, and (2) in equity for available-for-sale assets.

If, as a result of a change in intention or ability, it is no longer appropriate to classify an investment as held to maturity, it should be reclassified as available for sale and remeasured at fair value, with the difference between its carrying amount and fair value accounted for in equity. For a reclassification from the available-for-sale category to the held-to-maturity category, the fair value on the date of the reclassification becomes the new amortized cost basis, with any related gain or loss amortized over the investment's remaining life.

An impairment loss should be recognized for loans and receivables and held-to-maturity financial assets for the difference between the asset's carrying amount and the present value of estimated future cash flows. The carrying amount of the asset may be reduced either directly or through use of an allowance account. When an available-for-sale asset is deemed impaired, any decline in fair value previously recognized through equity should be removed therefrom and recognized in profit or loss for the current period; subsequently, if fair value of an available-for-sale investment increases, the impairment loss should be reversed (through profit or loss).

A financial asset should be derecognized when (1) the contractual rights to the cash flows from the financial asset expire, or (2) the contractual rights to receive the cash flows of the financial asset have been transferred. If, upon transfer, the entity retains the contractual rights to receive the cash flows of the financial asset but assumes a contractual obligation to pay the cash flows to one or more recipients, derecognition is appropriate if the arrangements meets the following conditions:

- The entity has no obligation to pay amounts to the eventual recipients unless it collects equivalent amounts from the original asset.

- The entity is prohibited by the terms of the transfer contract from selling or pledging the original asset other than as security to the eventual recipients for the obligation to pay them cash flows.

- The entity has an obligation to remit any cash flows it collects on behalf of the eventual recipients without material delay; in addition, the entity may not reinvest such cash flows, except for investments in cash or cash equivalents during the short settlement period from the collection date to the date of required remittance to the eventual recipients.

If substantially all the risks and rewards of ownership of the financial asset have been transferred, the difference between (1) the carrying amount and (2) the sum of the consideration received (including any new asset obtained less any new liability assumed) and any cumulative gain or loss that had been recognized directly in equity should be recognized in profit or loss.

## ¶ 310. Financial Liabilities

A financial liability should be initially measured at fair value; subsequently, all financial liabilities should be measured at amortized cost. A financial liability may be derecognized only when it is extinguished (i.e., when the obligation specified in the contract is discharged or cancelled or expires). The difference between (1) the carrying amount of a financial liability (or a part thereof) that has extinguished or transferred to another party, and (2) the consideration paid, including any non-cash assets transferred or liabilities assumed, should be recognized in profit or loss.

## ¶ 311. Financial Instruments with Characteristics of Both Debt and Equity

A liability is defined as a contractual obligation (1) to deliver cash or another financial asset to another entity, (2) to exchange financial assets or financial liabilities with another entity under conditions that are potentially unfavorable to the entity, or (3) that will or may be settled in the entity's own equity instruments. An instrument is considered a liability (rather than equity) unless it is not a contractual obligation. Instruments having such characteristics should be classified as liabilities, initially measured at fair value and subsequently at amortized cost.

## ¶ 312. The Fair Value Option

Upon initial recognition (and only then), any financial asset or liability (or group of financial assets or group of financial liabilities) may be designated to be measured at fair value, with changes in fair value recognized in profit or loss. Reclassifications into or out of such category are prohibited.

## ¶ 313. Troubled Debt Restructurings

The term "troubled debt restructuring" is not defined or referred to under IFRS. However, pursuant to IAS 39, an exchange between an existing borrower and lender of debt instruments with substantially different terms should be accounted for as an extinguishment of the original liability and recognition of a new liability. Similarly, a substantial modification of the terms of an existing liability or a portion of it (whether or not attributable to the financial difficulty of the debtor) should be accounted for as the simultaneous extinguishment of the original liability and the recognition of a new one.

Debt instruments are deemed to have substantially different terms if the discounted present value of the cash flows under the new terms (including any fees paid net of any fees received and discounted using the original effective interest rate) is at least 10% different from the discounted present value of the remaining cash flows of the original liability. If an exchange of debt instruments or modification of terms is accounted for as an extinguishment, any costs or fees incurred are recognized as part of the gain or loss on the extinguishment. If the exchange or modification is not accounted for as an extinguishment, any costs or fees incurred adjust the carrying amount of the liability and are amortized over the remaining term of the modified liability.

# ¶ 400. Inventories

## U.S. GAAP

## ¶ 401. Main Authoritative Sources

- ARB No. 43, *Restatement and Revision of Accounting Research Bulletins* (Chapter 4, "Inventory Pricing")

Inventories include the following:

- Finished goods.
- Work in process.
- Raw materials.
- Operating materials and supplies customarily classified as such by certain types of industries.

Inventories should be carried at cost, which, in the case of manufacturing or processing companies, includes a reasonable charge for overhead. Abnormal costs (e.g., double freight, re-handling, excess spoilage, idle facility) are required to be treated as current-period charges. Fixed production overhead should be allocated to inventories based on the normal capacity of the production facilities, with unallocated overhead charged to expense when incurred. If the utility of goods is impaired by damage, deterioration, obsolescence, changes in price levels, etc., a loss should be recognized in the period in which it occurs. The measurement of such loss is made by applying the lower-of-cost-or-market theory. The term "market" means current replacement cost (by purchase or manufacture), except that (1) market cannot exceed net realizable value (i.e., selling price less reasonable completion and disposal costs), and (2) market cannot be less than net realized value reduced by the company's normal profit margin. A write-down to lower of cost or market creates a new cost basis that may not be subsequently reversed.

Cost may be determined under any one of several methods. The most common methods are:

- Specific identification.
- First-in, first-out (FIFO).
- Last-in, first-out (LIFO).
- Average cost.

## IFRS

## ¶ 402. Main Authoritative Sources

- IAS 2, *Inventories*

Inventories are assets that are:

- Held for sale in the ordinary course of business.
- In the process of production for such sale.

- In the form of materials or supplies to be consumed in the production process or in the rendering of services.

Inventories should be measured at the lower of cost or net realizable value (i.e., selling price in the ordinary course of business less estimated costs of completion and selling costs). Cost comprises the cost of (1) purchase, (2) conversion, and (3) bringing inventories to their present location and condition. Cost of conversion includes the allocation of fixed production overheads based on the normal capacity of the production facilities. Abnormal costs (e.g., wasted materials, labor or other production costs) should be excluded from the cost of inventories and should be charged against current profit and loss.

Cost may be determined under one of the following methods (which must be consistently applied to all inventories of a similar nature and use):

- Specific identification.
- First-in, first-out (FIFO).
- Weighted-average.

If the cost of inventories is not recoverable due to damage, obsolescence, or the reduction of selling prices, a write-down to net realizable value is required. A new assessment of net realizable value must be made at each reporting date. When the circumstances that previously caused inventories to be written down below cost no longer exist, the amount of the write-down should be reversed (with the amount of the reversal limited to the amount of the original write-down).

# ¶ 500. Biological Assets

U.S. GAAP

## ¶ 501. Main Authoritative Sources

- ARB No. 43, *Restatement and Revision of Accounting Research Bulletins* (Chapter 4, "Inventory Pricing")
- SOP No. 85-3, *Accounting by Agricultural Producers and Agricultural Cooperatives*

The term "biological assets" does not, per se, exist in authoritative U.S. GAAP literature. The term is defined in IAS No. 41, *Agriculture*, as a living animal or plant. While no specific guidance exists under U.S. GAAP on accounting for biological assets, ARB No. 43 notes that only in exceptional cases may inventories properly be stated above cost (e.g., precious metals having a fixed monetary value with no substantial cost of marketing); any other exceptions must be justifiable by inability to determine appropriate approximate costs, immediate marketability at quoted market price, and the characteristic of unit interchangeability. SOP No. 85-3 permits animals available and held for sale and harvested crops to be accounted for either at (1) the lower of cost or market or (2) in accordance with established industry practice at sales price less estimated costs of disposal, when all of the following conditions exist:

- There are reliable, readily determinable and realizable market prices.
- The costs of disposal are relatively insignificant and predicable.
- The assets are available for immediate delivery.

IFRS

## ¶ 502. Main Authoritative Sources

- IAS 41, *Agriculture*

A biological asset or agricultural produce should be recognized only when:

- The entity controls the asset as a result of past events.
- It is probable that future economic benefits associated with the asset will flow to the entity.
- The fair value or cost of the asset can be measured reliably.

A biological asset is defined as a living animal or plant. Upon initial recognition and at each reporting date, a biological asset should be measured at fair value less estimated point-of-sale costs. A biological asset may be measured at cost less accumulated depreciation and accumulated impairment losses, however, if, upon initial recognition (1) market-determined prices or values are not available, and (2) alternative estimates of fair value are unreliable. Once the fair value of such a biological asset can be reliably determined, it should be measured at fair value less estimated point-of-sale costs.

Agricultural produce is defined as the harvested product of a biological asset. It should be measured at fair value less estimated point-of-sale costs at the point of harvest. Such measurement represents the cost at that date.

Any gain or loss arising on initial recognition of a biological asset at fair value less estimated point-of-sale costs (and from a change in fair value) should be included in the current period's profit or loss. A gain or loss arising on initial recognition of agricultural produce at fair value less estimated point-of-sale costs should also be included in profit or loss for the current period.

Note that IAS 41 does not apply to further processing of agricultural produce after harvest, at which time it is considered to be inventory. Thus, for example, IAS 41 applies to vines (the biological asset) and grapes (the agricultural produce from the vines), but it does not apply to wine (the product of processing after harvest).

# ¶ 600. Property, Plant, and Equipment

U.S. GAAP

## ¶ 601. Main Authoritative Sources

- ARB No. 43, *Restatement and Revision of Accounting Research Bulletins* (Chapter 9, "Depreciation")
- APB Opinion No. 6, *Status of Accounting Research Bulletins*

Property, plant, and equipment (PP&E) should be recorded at cost, which includes all expenditures directly related to the acquisition or construction of, and the preparations for, its intended use. Removal costs of structures on land acquired are usually added to the cost of the land rather than to the cost of the new structure. In connection with self-constructed assets, overhead should be allocated as an element of cost. Additions to PP&E that increase the service potential of the asset should be capitalized at cost; additions that are in substance repairs should be charged to operations when incurred. Ordinary repairs and maintenance should be expensed when incurred. A major repair should be capitalized if it benefits future periods.

When a component of PP&E is disposed of (regardless of the method of disposition), any gain or loss should be recognized in the period in which the disposition takes place. If an asset is abandoned without any cash being received, the loss is equal to the asset's book value. If a scrap (salvage) value exists, the gain or loss is the difference between the asset's scrap value and its book value. If an asset is still being used after it has been fully depreciated, the asset may remain in the accounts at no value (or at scrap value, if such a value exists).

PP&E is subject to impairment testing but should not be subsequently written up to reflect appraisal, market, or current values that are above cost.

## ¶ 602. Depreciation

Depreciation is a systematic allocation of the cost of PP&E (less scrap or salvage value, if any) over the estimated useful life of the asset. The objective of a depreciation method is to charge a portion of the cost of the PP&E to operations each year in order to match the revenue produced by the asset. Common depreciation methods include straight line (which is often used when no other method better matches cost with the asset's productivity) and the following accelerated methods that charge a greater portion of the asset's cost to operations in the earlier (and, theoretically, the more productive) years of an asset's life:

- Sum-of-the-years' digits.
- Declining balance (and double declining balance).
- Units of production.

IFRS

## ¶ 603. Main Authoritative Sources

- IAS 16, *Property, Plant and Equipment*

Property, plant, and equipment (PP&E) should be initially recorded at cost, which is the amount of cash or cash equivalents paid or the fair value of the other consideration given to acquire an asset at the time of its acquisition or construction. Initial cost also includes any costs directly attributable to bringing the asset to the location and condition necessary for it to be capable of operating in the manner intended by management. Subsequently, the cost of replacement parts is added to the carrying value of PP&E, but the costs of the day-to-day servicing of the item are charged to expense as incurred.

After initial recognition, PP&E may be carried either at (1) cost, less any accumulated depreciation and any accumulated impairment losses (i.e., the cost model), or at (2) a revalued amount, less any subsequent accumulated depreciation and subsequent accumulated impairment losses, if fair value can be reliably measured (i.e., the revaluation model). Revaluations should be made with sufficient regularity to ensure that the carrying amount of PP&E does not differ materially from that which would be determined using fair value at the balance sheet date. Note that, if an item of PP&E is revalued, the entire class to which that asset belongs must also be revalued.

If an asset's carrying amount is increased as a result of a revaluation, the increase should be credited directly to revaluation surplus in stockholders' equity. The increase should, however, be recognized in profit or loss to the extent that it reverses a revaluation decrease of the same asset previously recognized in profit or loss. If an asset's carrying amount is decreased as a result of a revaluation, the decrease should be recognized in profit or loss. However, the decrease should be charged directly to equity to the extent of any existing credit balance in the revaluation surplus in respect of that asset. The gain or loss arising from derecognition of PP&E should be included in profit or loss.

PP&E is subject to impairment testing; recognized impairment losses may, under certain circumstances, be reversed in subsequent periods.

## ¶ 604. Depreciation

The depreciable amount of an asset (which takes into account its estimated residual value) should be allocated on a systematic basis over the asset's useful life. The depreciation method used should reflect the pattern in which the asset's future economic benefits are expected to be consumed. Common methods include the straight-line method, the diminishing balance method, and the units of production method.

# ¶ 700. Intangibles

## U.S. GAAP

## ¶ 701. Main Authoritative Sources

- SFAS No. 2, *Accounting for Research and Development Costs*
- SFAS No. 68, *Research and Development Arrangements*
- SFAS No. 142, *Goodwill and Other Intangible Assets*
- SFAS No. 86, *Accounting for the Costs of Computer Software to Be Sold, Leased, or Otherwise Marketed*
- SOP 93-7, *Reporting on Advertising Costs*
- SOP 98-1, *Accounting for the Costs to Develop or Obtain Software for Internal Use*
- SOP 98-5, *Reporting on the Costs of Start-up Activities*
- EITF Issue No. 00-2, "Accounting for Web Site Development Costs"

## ¶ 702. In General

An acquired intangible asset (other than goodwill) should be recognized at fair value. The cost of acquiring a group of such assets should be allocated to individual assets on the basis of relative fair values. An intangible with a finite useful life should be amortized over that period (but not below its estimated residual value); an intangible with an indefinite life should not be amortized.

In a business combination, an intangible asset should be recognized (apart from goodwill) if the asset arises from contractual or other legal rights; if it does not arise from contractual or legal rights, it should be recognized only if it is separable (i.e., if it can be sold, transferred, licensed, rented, or exchanged).

Costs of internally developing, maintaining, or restoring intangible assets that are not specifically identifiable and that have indeterminate lives or that are inherent in a continuing business and related to the entity as a whole should be charged to operations when incurred.

For intangibles subject to amortization, an impairment loss is recognized if the carrying amount is not recoverable and the carrying amount exceeds its fair value. For intangibles not being amortized, the impairment test consists only of a comparison of the carrying amount with fair value (i.e., the recoverability condition is bypassed), with an impairment loss recognized if the carrying amount is greater than fair value. After an impairment loss has been recognized, the adjusted carrying amount of the asset represents its continuing basis of accounting (i.e., subsequent reversal of a previously recognized impairment loss is prohibited).

## ¶ 703. Advertising Costs

Advertising is defined as the promotion of an industry, a brand, product name, or specific products or services for the purpose of stimulating a positive image or for the purpose of creating or stimulating a desire to purchase the entity's products or services.

Advertising costs not qualifying as those associated with direct-response activities should be expensed as incurred or when the advertising first takes place (e.g., the initial showing of a television commercial or the first appearance of a magazine advertisement). The costs of advertising production (e.g., idea production, artwork, printing, audio and video crews) should be expensed as incurred. The cost of communication (e.g., airtime or space) should be reported as an expense after the airtime or space has been used.

The costs of billboards or blimps that are used for several advertising campaigns should be capitalized and amortized using a systematic and rational method over the expected useful lives of the related assets. Sales materials (e.g., brochures and catalogs) may be accounted for as prepaid supplies until they are no longer owned or expected to be used, at which time they should be expensed.

The costs of direct-response advertising should be capitalized if both of the following conditions are met:

- The primary purpose of the advertising is to elicit sales to customers who could be shown to have responded specifically to the advertising
- The direct-response advertising results in probable future benefits

Direct-response advertising costs that are not capitalized because it cannot be demonstrated that the direct-response advertising will result in future benefits should not be retroactively capitalized in subsequent periods if historical evidence in those subsequent periods indicates that the advertising did in fact result in future benefits.

Annual amortization of capitalized direct-response advertising costs should be based on the ratio of current-period primary revenue to the total of current and anticipated future-period revenue. The realizability of direct-response assets should be evaluated at each balance sheet date by comparing the carrying amounts of such assets to the probable remaining future net primary revenues expected to result directly from such advertising. For this evaluation, future net revenues are gross revenues less the probable future costs of all goods and activities necessary to earn those revenues, except for amortization of direct-response advertising. If the carrying amounts of such capitalized costs exceed the remaining future net revenues that probably will be realized, the excess should be reported as advertising expense in the current period. The reduced carrying amounts should not be adjusted upward if estimates of future net revenues are subsequently increased.

## ¶ 704. Computer Software Costs

All costs incurred to establish the technological feasibility of a computer software product to be sold, leased, or otherwise marketed are considered R&D costs and should be charged to operations as incurred. Technological feasibility is considered established when all planning, designing, coding (writing detailed instructions in computer language), and testing (steps to determine that the software meets the requirements set forth in the product design) activities have been performed.

Costs of producing a product master (a completed version of the software) incurred after establishing technological feasibility should be capitalized; these costs include coding and testing. Software production costs for software that is to be used as an integral part of a product or process should not be capitalized until (1) technological feasibility has been established for the software, and (2) all R&D activities for the other components of the product or process have been completed. Capitalization should stop when the product is available for general release to customers. Costs of customer support should be charged to operations when the related revenue is recognized or when the costs are incurred, whichever occurs first. Costs of purchased computer software that has no alternative future use should be accounted for in the same manner as the costs incurred to internally develop such software. If the purchased software has an alternative future use, the cost should be capitalized and accounted for in accordance with its use.

Capitalized software costs should be amortized on a product-by-product basis. Amortization should begin when the product is available to customers. The amount of amortization each year should be the larger of the amount computed using either:

- The ratio that current gross revenues for a product bear to the total of current and anticipated future gross revenues for that product, or
- The straight-line method over the remaining estimated economic life of the product including the period being reported on.

Software is considered internal use software if (1) the software is acquired, internally developed, or modified solely to meet the entity's internal needs, and (2) during the software's development or modification, no plan exists to market the software externally.

In general, computer software development occurs in the following stages:

- Preliminary project stage.
- Application development stage.
- Post-implementation/operation stage.

Both internal and external costs incurred during the preliminary project stage should be charged to operations as incurred. Such costs incurred during the application development stage should be capitalized. Training costs incurred in the application development stage should, however, be expensed. Costs of upgrades and enhancements should be capitalized (but only during the application development stage) if it is probable that the expenditures will result in added functionality for the software. During the post-implementation/operation stage, training costs (both internal and external) and maintenance costs should be charged to operations.

Capitalization of costs should begin when (1) the preliminary project stage is completed, and (2) management with the relevant authority permits and commits to funding a computer software project and believes the completion of the project is probable and the software will be used to perform the function intended.

Capitalization should be discontinued when (1) it is no longer probable that the project will be completed and placed in service, or (2) the project is substantially completed and ready for its intended use. Only the following costs should be capitalized:

- External direct costs of materials and services consumed in developing or obtaining internal use computer software.
- Payroll and payroll related costs for employees who are directly associated with and who devote time to the internal use computer software project, to the extent of the time spent directly on the project.
- Interest costs incurred during development of internal use computer software.

Impairment should be tested under any of the following conditions:

- Internal-use computer software is not expected to provide substantive service potential.
- A significant change occurs in the extent or manner in which the software is used or is expected to be used.
- A significant change is made or will be made to the software program.
- Costs of developing or modifying internal use computer software significantly exceed the amount originally expected for such activities.

When it is no longer probable that computer software being developed will be completed and placed in service, the asset should be reported at the lower of the carrying amount or fair value, if any, less costs to sell (with the rebuttable presumption that the fair value is zero).

Amortization of capitalized costs should be taken on the straight-line basis unless another method is more representative of the software's use. Amortization should begin when the software is ready for its intended use, even if it will be placed in service in stages that extend beyond the current reporting period.

## ¶ 705. Web Site Development Costs

Generally, web site development costs relating to application, infrastructure development, and graphics development should be accounted for in the same manner as computer software costs, which depends on whether the web site is to be sold or is intended for internal use. All costs incurred in the planning stage should be charged to current earnings, and fees incurred for web site hosting should be expensed over the period of benefit.

## ¶ 706. Research and Development Costs

All research and development (R&D) costs should be charged to expense when incurred, except for costs of certain elements that are expected to have alternative future uses. In connection with an arrangement under which research and development is funded by others, the company must determine whether it is obligated only to perform contractual research and development or whether it is otherwise obligated. To the extent that the company is obligated to repay the other parties, it should record a liability and charge the related R&D costs to expense when incurred.

The term "research" is defined as:

- The planned search or critical investigation aimed at discovery of new knowledge with the hope that such knowledge will be useful in developing a new product or service or a new process or technique or in bringing about significant improvement to an existing product or process.

The term "development" is defined as:

- The translation of research findings or other knowledge into a plan or design for a new product or process or for a significant improvement to an existing product or process whether intended for sale or use. It includes the conceptual formulation, design and testing of product alternatives, construction of prototypes, and operation of pilot plants. It does not include routine or periodic alterations to existing products, production lines, manufacturing processes, and other ongoing operations, even though those alterations may represent improvements, and it also does not include market research or market-testing activities.

## ¶ 707. Start-Up Costs

Start-up activities are defined as one-time activities related to opening a new facility, introducing a new product or service, conducting business in a new territory or with a new class of customer, initiating a new process in an existing facility, or commencing some new operation. Start-up activities do not include activities related to routine, ongoing efforts to refine, enrich, or otherwise improve the qualities of an existing product, service, process, or facility; nor are activities related to a merger or acquisition or to continuing customer acquisition considered start-up activities. Costs of start-up activities, including organization costs, should be charged to operations as incurred.

IFRS

## ¶ 708. Main Authoritative Sources

- IAS 38, *Intangible Assets*
- SIC 32, *Intangible Assets—Web Site Costs*

## ¶ 709. In General

An intangible asset should be recognized if (1) it is probable that the expected future economic benefits attributable to the asset will flow to the entity, and (2) the cost of the asset can be measured reliably. Initial measurement of an intangible asset should be at cost. The cost of a separately acquired intangible asset comprises the purchase price and costs directly attributable to preparing the asset for its intended use. Cost of an intangible asset acquired in a business combination is the asset's fair value at the date of acquisition.

After recognition, intangible assets may be carried either at (1) cost less accumulated amortization and accumulated impairment losses (i.e., the cost model), or (2) a revalued amount equal to fair value at the date of the revaluation less subsequent accumulated amortization and subsequent accumulated impairment losses (i.e., the revaluation model). Revaluations should be made with sufficient regularity so that, at the balance sheet date, the carrying amount of the asset does not differ materially from its fair value. Note that, if an intangible asset in a class of revalued intangible assets cannot be revalued because there is no active market for this asset, the carrying amount of the asset should be based on application of the cost model.

An increase in an intangible asset's carrying amount under the revaluation model should be credited directly to revaluation surplus in stockholders' equity. To the extent, however, that the increase reverses a previously recognized revaluation decrease in profit and loss for the same asset, the increase should be recognized in profit and loss.

A decrease resulting from revaluation should be recognized in profit and loss, but should be charged directly to revaluation surplus in equity to the extent of any remaining revaluation surplus attributable to the same asset.

An intangible asset with a finite useful life should be amortized over its useful life; an intangible asset with an indefinite useful life should not be amortized. Internally generated goodwill should not be recognized as an asset; neither should internally generated brands, mastheads, publishing titles, customer lists, and items similar in substance. Costs related to such items should be charged to operations when incurred.

## ¶ 710. Advertising Costs

IFRS does not directly address accounting for advertising costs.

## ¶ 711. Computer Software Costs

Although IFRS does not specifically refer to accounting for computer software to be sold, leased, or otherwise marketed, the costs to generate a potential intangible asset should be classified either as research or development. All expenditures in the research phase should be charged to profit and loss. Costs incurred for development should be capitalized as an intangible asset only if the following can be demonstrated:

- The technical feasibility of completing the intangible asset so that it will be available for use or sale.

- The intention to complete the intangible asset and use or sell it.

- The ability to use or sell the intangible asset.

- The manner in which the intangible asset will generate probable future economic benefits.

- The availability of adequate technical, financial, and other resources to complete the development and to use or sell the intangible asset.

- The ability to measure reliably the expenditure attributable to the intangible asset during its development.

## ¶ 712. Web Site Development Costs

Costs associated with the development and operation of an entity's own web site should be accounted for as follows:

- Costs incurred in the planning stage should be charged to profit or loss.

- Costs incurred in the application and infrastructure development stage, in the graphical design stage, and in the content design stage for the purpose of advertising or promoting the entity's products or services should be expensed immediately; other costs in such stages may be capitalized as an asset if the expenditures can be directly attributed and are necessary to create, produce or prepare the web site for it to be capable of operating in the manner intended by management.

- Costs incurred in the operating stage should generally be charged to profit and loss, unless such costs otherwise qualify as an intangible asset and it is probable that the expected future economic benefits that are attributable to the asset will flow to the entity.

## ¶ 713. Research and Development Costs

Research is defined as the original and planned investigation undertaken with the prospect of gaining new scientific or technical knowledge and understanding. Development is defined as the application of research findings or other knowledge to a plan or design for the production of new or substantially improved materials, devices, products, processes, systems or services before the start of commercial production or use.

Costs of research (or on the research phase of an internal project) should be recognized as an expense when it is incurred. An intangible asset arising from development (or from the development phase of an internal project) should be recognized only if the following can be demonstrated:

- The technical feasibility of completing the intangible asset so that it will be available for use or sale.

- The intention to complete the intangible asset and use or sell it.

- The ability to use or sell the intangible asset.

- The manner in which the intangible asset will generate probable future economic benefits.

- The availability of adequate technical, financial, and other resources to complete the development and to use or sell the intangible asset.

- The ability to measure reliably the expenditure attributable to the intangible asset during its development

If it is not possible to distinguish between the research phase and the development phase of an internal project to create an intangible asset, the entire cost of that project should be treated as if it were incurred in the research phase only (i.e., charged to profit and loss as incurred).

## ¶ 714. Start-Up Costs

Start-up costs represent expenditures that are intended to provide future economic benefits to an entity, but no intangible asset or other asset is acquired or created that qualifies for recognition. Accordingly, such costs should be charged to profit and loss as incurred (unless they for a part of the cost of an item of property, plant, and equipment).

# ¶ 800. Impairment of Long-Lived Assets

## U.S. GAAP

## ¶ 801. Main Authoritative Sources

- SFAS No. 142, *Goodwill and Other Intangible Assets*
- SFAS No. 144, *Accounting for the Impairment or Disposal of Long-Lived Assets*

## ¶ 802. Other Than Goodwill

A long-lived asset (or asset group) that is held and used is considered impaired when its carrying amount is not recoverable and it exceeds the asset's fair value. The carrying amount is deemed unrecoverable if it is greater than the sum of undiscounted cash flows expected to result from use and eventual disposition of the asset. An impairment loss is equal to the excess of the carrying amount over the fair value of the asset (or group). Thus, once it is determined that carrying value will not be recovered, an impairment loss must be recognized.

The carrying amount of the asset being tested for impairment should include capitalized asset retirement costs. Estimated future cash flows related to the asset retirement obligation should not, however, be included in the amounts of undiscounted cash inflows and the present value of cash inflows (i.e., to estimate fair value) when testing for recoverability or when measuring the impairment loss.

A long-lived asset held and used should be tested for recoverability when events or changes in circumstances indicate that its carrying value may exceed future undiscounted cash inflows. Such events or changes in circumstances include the following:

- A significant decrease in the market price of the asset.
- A significant adverse change in the degree or manner in which the asset is being used.
- A significant deterioration in the asset's physical condition.
- A significant adverse change in legal factors (including actions or assessments by regulators) or in the business climate that could affect the asset's value.
- An accumulation of costs significantly exceeding the amount originally anticipated for the acquisition or construction of the asset.
- A cash flow deficit or an operating loss in the current period, which, when combined with a history of such deficits or losses, indicates future ongoing losses associated with the use of the asset.
- The expectation that it is more likely than not that the asset will be sold or otherwise disposed of well in advance of its previously estimated useful life.

For purposes of testing for recoverability and measuring an impairment loss, individual long-lived assets held and used should be grouped with other assets (and liabilities) forming the lowest level for which identifiable cash flows are largely independent of those of the entity's other assets and liabilities. If an impairment loss is recognized, it should be applied only to the long-lived assets in the group that are covered by SFAS No. 144; thus, other assets in the group are not affected but should, if necessary, be adjusted for impairment in accordance with other applicable GAAP.

Goodwill should be part of an asset group to be tested for impairment only if the group is itself a reporting unit or includes such a unit. A reporting unit is an operating segment or a level just below that of a segment. When testing for impairment of a group that is at a level lower than that of a reporting unit (and thus does not include goodwill), estimates of future cash flows of that group should not be adjusted for the impact of having excluded goodwill. The carrying amounts of other assets in the group (i.e., those not covered by SFAS No. 144) and liabilities in that group should, however, be adjusted for impairment in accordance with applicable authoritative pronouncements before testing for impairment pursuant to SFAS No. 144.

If an impairment loss is recognized, it should be applied only to the covered long-lived assets in the group. Allocation of the loss should be pro rata, based on relative carrying amounts; in no instance, however, may an individual long-lived asset in the group be reduced to a carrying amount below the asset's fair value (if that fair value is determinable without undue cost and effort). Once an impairment loss is recorded, the written-down carrying amount of a long-lived asset becomes its new cost basis (and, if applicable, depreciated or amortized over its estimated useful life).

## ¶ 803. Goodwill

Goodwill arising in a business combination should not be amortized but is subject to impairment testing at the reporting unit level. At the date of the business combination, all goodwill must be assigned to one or more reporting units. A reporting unit is defined as an operating segment or one level below that of a segment. Goodwill should be assigned to reporting units that are expected to benefit from the synergies of the business combination—even though other acquired assets or liabilities assumed have not been assigned to that unit. Conceptually, the amount of goodwill assigned to a specific reporting unit is determined in a manner similar to the way goodwill is determined in a business combination itself. Thus, the fair value of each reporting unit represents a "purchase price equivalent," which is to be allocated to the various assets and liabilities of that unit. If the hypothetical purchase price exceeds the aggregate amount assigned, the excess is considered goodwill attributable to that unit. If, however, a unit has not been assigned any of the acquired net assets, goodwill is determined as the difference between the unit's overall fair value before and after the acquisition (referred to as the "with-and-without" calculation).

Testing for impairment of goodwill is performed in two steps:

- Potential impairment is identified by comparing the fair value of a reporting unit with its carrying amount (including goodwill).
- If fair value is less than the carrying amount, an impairment loss is estimated as the excess of the carrying amount of the goodwill over its implied value.

Implied fair value of a reporting unit's goodwill is determined by allocating the fair value of the entire unit to all of the unit's assets and liabilities; any excess of fair value over the amount allocated represents implied fair value of that unit's goodwill. Note that the allocation process is performed solely for purposes of testing goodwill for impairment. Thus, the carrying amounts of assets and liabilities are not affected.

Fair value of a unit represents the price that would be received for such unit in an orderly transaction between market participants at the measurement date. Although quoted prices in an active market are the best evidence of fair value, the market capitalization of a unit's publicly traded equity securities may not be reflective of the unit's fair value (i.e., because a buyer may be willing to pay more for the unit to serve the buyer's specific purpose for acquiring it).

Testing for a unit's goodwill impairment must be performed at least annually at any time during the year (but at the same time each year); different reporting units may be tested at different dates. Impairment testing should take place more frequently, however, if an event occurs or circumstances change that would more likely than not reduce a unit's fair value below its carrying amount.

When a reporting unit is to be disposed of, goodwill of that unit should be included in the carrying amount in determining gain or loss on disposal. When only a portion of a reporting unit that constitutes a business is to be disposed of, the amount of goodwill assigned to the portion being disposed of (for purposes of computing gain or loss) should be based on the relative fair values of (1) the business to be disposed of, and (2) the remaining portion of the reporting unit.

IFRS

## ¶ 804. Main Authoritative Sources

- IAS 36, *Impairment of Assets*

## ¶ 805. Other Than Goodwill

An asset is impaired when its carrying amount exceeds its recoverable amount. At each reporting date, an assessment should be made to determine whether there is any indication that an asset may be impaired; if any such indication exists, the recoverable amount of the asset should be estimated. Regardless of whether such indication exists, an impairment test must be made annually of intangible assets with indefinite useful lives (i.e., those not subject to amortization).

Indicators of possible impairment include the following:

- An asset's market value has declined significantly more than would be expected as a result of the passage of time or normal use.

- Significant changes with an adverse effect on the entity have taken place during the period, or will take place in the near future, in the technological, market, economic, or legal environment in which the entity operates or in the market to which an asset is dedicated.

- Market interest rates or other market rates of return on investments have increased during the period, and those increases are likely to affect the discount rate used in calculating an asset's value in use and decrease the asset's recoverable amount materially.

- The carrying amount of the net assets of the entity is more than its market value.

- Evidence is available of obsolescence or physical damage of an asset.

- Significant changes with an adverse effect on the entity have taken place during the period or are expected to take place in the near future in the extent to which or manner in which an asset is used or is expected to be used.

- Evidence is available from internal reporting indicating that the economic performance of an asset is or will be worse than expected.

An asset's recoverable amount is the greater of its (1) fair value less costs to sell, and (2) value in use (i.e., the present value of the future cash flows expected to be derived from the asset). An impairment loss should be recognized when an asset's carrying amount is less than its recoverable amount. If it is not possible to estimate the recoverable amount of an individual asset, such amount should be determined for the cash-generating unit to which the asset belongs. A cash-generating unit is defined as the smallest identifiable group of assets generating cash inflows that are largely independent of the cash inflows from other assets or groups of assets.

## ¶ 806. Goodwill

For the purpose of impairment testing, goodwill acquired in a business combination must be allocated to each of the acquirer's cash-generating units that is expected to benefit from the synergies of the combination (irrespective of whether other acquired assets or liabilities are assigned to those units). A cash-generating unit to which goodwill has been allocated should be tested for impairment annually (at the same time during the year) and whenever else an indication exists that the unit may be impaired by comparing the carrying amount of the unit (including the goodwill) with the recoverable amount of the unit. If the carrying amount of the unit exceeds its recoverable amount, an impairment loss should be recognized and allocated to the carrying amount of the assets of the unit (1) to reduce the carrying amount of any goodwill allocated to the cash-generating unit, and (2) to the other assets of the unit pro rata on the basis of the carrying amount of each asset in the unit. Note, though, that an individual asset's carrying amount may not be reduced below the highest of its fair value, less costs to sell, its value in use, or zero.

A previously recognized impairment loss for an individual asset (other than goodwill) may be subsequently reversed (if circumstances have changed); a previously recognized impairment loss for goodwill, however, may not be subsequently reversed.

# ¶ 900. Non-Current Assets Held for Sale

### U.S. GAAP

## ¶ 901. Main Authoritative Sources

- SFAS No. 144, *Accounting for the Impairment or Disposal of Long-Lived Assets*

A long-lived asset (or group of assets, which, in this context, is referred to as the "disposal group") to be sold should be classified as held for sale in the period that all of the following criteria are met:

- Management having the authority to do so commits to a plan to sell the asset (or disposal group).

- The asset is available for immediate sale in its present condition, subject only to terms and conditions that are usual and customary for sales of such assets.

- An active program to locate a buyer has been initiated, and other actions required to complete the plan of sale have been undertaken.

- Sale of the asset is probable and transfer of the asset is normally expected to qualify for accounting recognition as a sale within one year's time.

- The asset is being actively marketed for sale at a price that is reasonable in relation to its current fair value.

- It is unlikely that significant changes to the plan of sale will be made or that the plan itself will be withdrawn.

A newly acquired asset should be classified (as of the acquisition date) as held for sale only if (1) the one-year expected selling period is met, and (2) all other criteria for held-for-sale classification are met (or it is probable that they will be met within three months' time).

An asset (or disposal group) should be measured at the lesser of (1) its carrying amount, or (2) fair value, less costs to sell it. A newly acquired asset should be measured at fair value (which is presumptively the purchase price), less costs to sell. An asset otherwise subject to depreciation or amortization should not be depreciated or amortized while it is classified as held for sale, but interest or other expenses attributable to liabilities of the disposal group should continue to be accrued.

An impairment loss representing the excess of the carrying amount of an asset (group) held for sale over its fair value (less costs to sell) should be recognized. Subsequent increases in fair value (less costs to sell) should also be recognized but not in an amount greater than the total of previously recognized impairment losses (i.e., gains are limited to the recovery of previous losses).

When the decision is made not to sell a long-lived asset (or group) previously held for sale, the asset should be reclassified as held and used. Initial measurement after the reclassification should be at the lesser of (1) the asset's carrying amount before it was held for sale, less depreciation or amortization that would have been recognized, or (2) fair value at the date of the subsequent decision not to sell. Any resulting loss on the reclassification should be immediately recognized.

If an individual asset (or liability) is removed from a disposal group, the other assets and liabilities should continue to be measured as a group only if all the criteria for classification as held for sale are still satisfied. Otherwise, the remaining long-lived assets should be measured individually at the lower of their respective carrying amounts or fair values, less costs to sell; the long-lived asset that was removed from the group should be measured at the lesser of its carrying amount before classification as held for sale (adjusted for the amount of foregone depreciation or amortization) or its fair value at the date of the reclassification.

A long-lived asset to be disposed of in any manner other than by sale should continue to be classified as held and used until the disposition actually occurs. If an entity commits to a plan of abandonment before the end of an asset's previously expected useful life, depreciation expense should be revised accordingly. Note that a temporarily idled asset is not considered to be abandoned.

The gain or loss realized upon the sale or other disposition of an individual long-lived asset (or of a disposal group not rising to the level of a component and thus not qualifying as a discontinued operation) should be reported as part of income from continuing operations. Assets and liabilities of a disposal group should be shown separately in the balance sheet (i.e., they may not be offset or shown on a net basis).

IFRS

## ¶ 902. Main Authoritative Sources

- IFRS 5, *Non-Current Assets Held for Sale and Discontinued Operations*

A non-current asset (or disposal group) should be classified as held for sale if its carrying amount will be recovered principally through a sale rather than through continuing use. The asset (or disposal group) must be available for immediate sale in its present condition subject only to terms that are usual and customary for sales of such assets and the sale must be highly probable (i.e., the appropriate level of management must be committed to a plan to sell the asset and an active program to locate a buyer and complete the plan must have been initiated). In addition, the asset must be actively marketed for sale at a price that is reasonable in relation to its current fair value; the sale should be expected to be completed within one year from the date of classification. A non-current asset (or disposal group) to be abandoned should not be classified as held for sale.

A non-current asset (or disposal group) classified as held for sale should be measured at the lower of its carrying amount and fair value less costs to sell. If a newly acquired asset meets the criteria to be classified as held for sale, the asset should be measured on initial recognition at the lower of its carrying amount had it not been so classified (e.g., cost) and fair value less costs to sell.

An impairment loss should be recognized for the initial or subsequent write-down of the asset to fair value less costs to sell; a gain should be recognized for any subsequent increase in fair value less costs to sell of an asset, but not in excess of the cumulative impairment loss previously recorded.

A non-current asset that ceases to be classified as held for sale (or ceases to be included in a disposal group classified as held for sale) should be measured at the lower of (1) its carrying amount before the asset (or disposal group) was classified as held for sale, adjusted for any depreciation, amortization, or revaluations that would have been recognized had the asset (or disposal group) not been classified as held for sale, and (2) its recoverable amount at the date of the subsequent decision not to sell.

If an individual asset (or liability) is removed from a disposal group classified as held for sale, the remaining assets and liabilities of the disposal group to be sold should continue to be measured as a group if all the conditions for classification as held for sale are met; the remaining non-current assets of the group that individually meet the criteria to be classified as held for sale should be measured individually at the lower of their carrying amounts and fair values less costs to sell at that date.

Assets and liabilities held for sale should be shown separately in the balance sheet from other assets and liabilities (and may not be offset).

# ¶ 1000. Investments in Associated Entities

### U.S. GAAP

## ¶ 1001. Main Authoritative Sources

- APB Opinion No. 18, *The Equity Method of Accounting for Investments in Common Stock*
- FASB Interpretation No. 35, *Criteria for Applying the Equity Method of Accounting for Investments in Common Stock*
- EITF Issue No. 00-1, "Investor Balance Sheet and Income Statement Display under the Equity Method for Investments in Certain Partnerships and Other Ventures"

The equity method should be used to account for investments, corporate joint ventures, and other investments in common stock if the investor has the ability to exercise significant influence over the operating and financial policies of the investee. When the equity method is not appropriate, the investment should be accounted for pursuant to SFAS No. 115, *Accounting for Certain Investments in Debt and Equity Securities* or pursuant to the cost method for investments in equity securities that do not have readily determinable fair values.

Under the cost method, a long-term investment is recorded at cost and carried at that amount until it is sold or otherwise disposed of or until it is written down for an impairment loss or when dividends received represent a liquidating dividend (i.e., a dividend received in excess of earnings subsequent to the investment date). A cost-method investment is deemed impaired when its fair value is below cost. If impairment is considered other than temporary, an impairment loss should be recognized as the difference between the investment's cost and its fair value as of the end of the reporting period. After recognition of the impairment loss, the fair value to which the investment has been written down becomes its new cost basis (which should not be upwardly adjusted for subsequent partial or complete recovery of the fair value deficiency).

Determining the investor's ability to exercise significant influence requires judgment to assess the status of each investment. An investment (direct or indirect) of 20% or more of the voting stock of an investee is presumed, however, in the absence of evidence to the contrary, to be sufficient for an investor to have the ability to exercise significant influence over an investee. Conversely, unless such ability can be demonstrated, an investment of less than 20% leads to the presumption that the investor does not have the ability to influence significantly an investee.

Generally, under the equity method, the investor records its proportionate share of the investee's income or loss for the period. The carrying value of an equity-method investment is cost plus the accumulated amount of the investor's share of the investee's profit (or minus the accumulated amount of the investor's share of the investee's losses) less dividends received from the investee. As is the case with a consolidated subsidiary, (1) intercompany transactions and balances are eliminated, (2) any excess of the carrying value of the investment over the book value of the investee's net assets is allocated to specific assets (and liabilities), which, if applicable, should be depreciated or amortized over their useful lives, and (3) any unidentified excess is considered to be goodwill. An impairment loss should be recognized when the fair value of the investment is less than its carrying value (and the loss is deemed to be other than temporary).

If an investor's share of losses of an investee equals or exceeds the carrying amount of the investment (plus advances made by the investor), application of the equity method should ordinarily be discontinued when the investment (plus net advances) is reduced to zero. Additional losses should not be recognized, unless the investor has guaranteed obligations of the investee or is otherwise committed to provide further financial support for the investee. If the investee subsequently reports net income, the investor should resume applying the equity method but only after its share of that net income equals the share of net losses not recognized during the period the equity method was suspended.

If the criteria for applying the equity method are subsequently met for an investment previously accounted for either in accordance with SFAS No. 115 or on the cost method, the investment account, results of operations, and retained earnings should be adjusted retroactively in a manner consistent with the accounting for a step-by-step acquisition of a subsidiary. If, however, the level of ownership falls below 20% or the investor otherwise loses significant influence over the investee, the equity method should cease being applied, but the investment account (and previous results of operations) should not be retroactively adjusted.

A proportionate gross financial statement presentation (i.e., proportionate consolidation) is not appropriate for an investment in an unincorporated legal entity accounted for by the equity method, unless the investee is in either the construction industry or an extractive industry in which there is a longstanding practice of its use. If, however, the investor/venturer (1) holds an undivided interest in each asset, (2) is proportionately liable for each liability, and (3) no other separate legal entity exists, the investor may display, on a proportionate gross basis, those assets and liabilities and the related results of operations on a proportionate gross basis.

IFRS

## ¶ 1002. Main Authoritative Sources

- IAS 28, *Investments in Associates*
- IAS 31, *Interests in Joint Ventures*

An associated entity (referred to simply as an associate) is one over which the investor has significant influence and such entity is neither a subsidiary nor an interest in a joint venture. Significant influence is defined as the power to participate in the financial and operating policy decisions of the investee and is presumed to exist for an investment of 20% or more of the voting power; likewise, significant influence is presumed not to exist for an investment of less than 20% of the voting power, although both presumptions are rebuttable if clear evidence demonstrates otherwise.

When an investor has significant influence, it must account for its investment by the equity method. Under the equity method, the investment in an associate is initially recognized at cost and the carrying amount is increased or decreased for the investor's share of the profit or loss of the investee after the date of acquisition. Distributions received from an investee reduce the carrying amount of the investment. Many of the procedures appropriate for the application of the equity method are similar to consolidation procedures, as follows:

- Intercompany transactions and balances are eliminated.

- The excess of the cost of the investment over the book value of the investor's proportionate share of the investee's net assets is allocated to specific assets and liabilities; if applicable, such excess should be depreciated or amortized over the useful lives of the assets to which it was assigned.

- Any remaining excess over allocated fair values should be considered goodwill.

An impairment loss should be recognized if the carrying amount of the investment is greater than its recoverable amount.

An investor should discontinue the use of the equity method from the date it ceases to have significant influence over an associate. The carrying amount of the investment as of the date that it ceases to be an associate should be regarded as its cost on initial measurement as a financial asset.

If an investor's share of losses of an associate equals or exceeds its interest in the associate, the investor should discontinue recognizing further losses. After the investor's interest is reduced to zero, additional losses should be provided for (and a liability recognized) to the extent that the investor has incurred legal or constructive obligations or made payments on behalf of the associate. If the associate subsequently reports profits, the investor should resume recognizing its share of such profits only after its share of the profits equals the share of losses previously not recognized.

IFRS 31 distinguishes among three types of joint ventures: (1) jointly controlled operations; (2) jointly controlled assets; and (3) jointly controlled entities. In respect of its interest in a jointly controlled operation, a venturer should recognize in its financial statements:

- The assets it controls and the liabilities it incurs.

- The expenses it incurs and its share of the income it earns from the sale of goods or services by the joint venture.

In respect of an interest in jointly controlled assets, a venturer should recognize in its financial statements:

- Its share of the jointly controlled assets, classified according to the nature of the assets.

- Any liabilities it has incurred.

- Its share of any liabilities incurred jointly with the other venturers.

- Any income from the sale or use of its share of the output of the joint venture, together with its share of any expenses incurred by the joint venture.
- Any expenses it has incurred related its interest in the joint venture.

A venturer in a jointly controlled entity may account for its interest either using proportionate consolidation (i.e., the benchmark treatment) or the equity method (i.e., the alternative allowed treatment). Application of proportionate consolidation means that the balance sheet of the venturer will include its share of the assets it controls jointly and its share of the liabilities for which it is jointly responsible; the income statement of the venturer using proportionate consolidation will include its share of the income and expenses of the jointly controlled entity.

# ¶ 1100 . Investment Property

U.S. GAAP

## ¶ 1101. Main Authoritative Sources

- None—not directly addressed

There is no specific guidance under U.S. GAAP concerning the accounting treatment of investment property, which is defined by IFRS as land or buildings held by the owner or by a lessee (under a capital lease) for the purpose of earning rental income on such property or for capital appreciation.

IFRS

## ¶ 1102. Main Authoritative Sources

- IAS 40, *Investment Property*

Investment property is defined as land or buildings held by the owner or by a lessee under a finance (i.e., capital) lease for the purpose of earning rental income on such property or for capital appreciation, rather than for: (1) use in the production or supply of goods or services or for administrative purposes, or (2) sale in the ordinary course of business.

Note, though, that a property interest held by a lessee under an *operating* lease may be classified and accounted for as investment property if the property would otherwise meet the definition of an investment property and the lessee uses the fair value model to account for the asset. This classification alternative is available on a property-by-property basis; once this classification alternative is selected, however, for one such property interest held under an operating lease, all property classified as investment property must be accounted for using the fair value model.

Investment property should be recognized as an asset when (1) it is probable that the future economic benefits associated with the investment property will flow to the entity, and (2) the cost of the investment property can be measured reliably. Initially, investment property should be measured at cost. Initial cost of investment property held under a finance lease is equal to the lower of the fair value of the property and the present value of the minimum lease payments, with a corresponding amount recognized as a liability.

Subsequently, investment property may be measured by applying either the cost model or the fair value model (except in the case of investment property held under an operating lease, for which the fair value model must be used). Under the fair value model, any change in fair value should be recognized immediately in profit and loss.

There is a rebuttable presumption that the fair value of an investment property can be reliably determined on a continuing basis. If, however, in exceptional cases, when an entity first acquires an investment property (or when an existing property first becomes investment property following the completion of construction or development), comparable market transactions are infrequent and alternative reliable estimates of fair value (e.g., based on discounted cash flow projections) are not available, the cost model should be used. Once investment property is measured at fair value, it must continue to be measured at fair value until disposal (or until the property becomes owner-occupied or it is being developed for subsequent sale in the ordinary course of business), even if comparable market transactions become less frequent or market prices become less readily available.

For a transfer from inventories to investment property that will be carried at fair value, any difference between the fair value of the property at the transfer date and its previous carrying amount should be recognized in profit or loss. For a transfer from investment property carried at fair value to owner-occupied property or to inventories, the property's deemed cost for subsequent accounting should be its fair value at the date of change in use. An investment property should be derecognized upon disposal or when the investment property is permanently withdrawn from use and no future economic benefits are expected from its disposal.

# ¶ 1200. Stockholders' Equity

## U.S. GAAP

## ¶ 1201. Main Authoritative Sources

- ARB No. 43, *Restatement and Revision of Accounting Research Bulletins* (Chapter 7A, "Quasi-Reorganization and Corporate Adjustment")
- ARB No. 43, *Restatement and Revision of Accounting Research Bulletins* (Chapter 7B, "Stock Dividends and Stock Split-ups")
- APB Opinion No. 6, *Status of Accounting Research Bulletins*
- APB Opinion No. 14, *Accounting for Convertible Debt Issues with Stock Purchase Warrants*
- APB Opinion No. 29, *Accounting for Nonmonetary Transactions*
- SFAS No. 84, *Induced Conversions of Convertible Debt*
- SFAS No. 150, *Accounting for Certain Financial Instruments with Characteristics of Both Debt and Equity*

**Note:** U.S. GAAP does not directly (and generally) address the recognition and measurement of stockholders' equity nor of its various components as separate accounting issues. Thus, following is a discussion only of selected matters.

## ¶ 1202. Warrants and Convertible Instruments

When stock warrants are sold separately (i.e., not attached to any other security), the amount of cash proceeds from the sale is credited to additional paid-in capital. When preferred stock is issued with warrants that are not detachable from preferred stock, the market value of the preferred stock and the stock warrants are inseparable. In such a case, all proceeds received on the sale are allocated to the preferred stock and the accounting is identical to any other issue of stock. When the warrants are detachable, the price of the combined security should be allocated to the preferred stock and the warrants based on their relative market values at the time they are issued.

When convertible debt is issued, no accounting recognition is given to the conversion feature. At conversion, either the market value or book value method may be used. Under the market value method, a gain or loss may occur. Under the book value method, the stock issued upon conversion is recorded at the carrying value of the converted bonds. When the terms of conversion of convertible debt have been altered to induce conversion, an expense equal to the fair value of the incremental consideration (the inducement or "sweetener") should be recorded.

## ¶ 1203. Redeemable Preferred Stock

Mandatorily redeemable preferred stock should be classified as a liability if it requires the issuer to redeem the stock by transferring assets at specified or determinable dates upon an event certain to occur, unless redemption is mandatory only upon the liquidation or termination of the entity. Mandatorily redeemable preferred stock should be shown in the balance sheet as a liability (i.e., not as equity nor positioned between liabilities and stockholders' equity). In general, mandatorily re-deemable preferred stock should be measured initially at fair value, with subsequent changes in fair value recognized in current earnings.

## ¶ 1204. Stock Dividends and Splits

A stock dividend does not result in any changes in the company's assets or the respective proportionate interests of the stockholders. A stock dividend is accounted for by a charge to retained earnings for the fair value of the additional shares issued and corresponding credits to common stock and additional paid-in capital. Where the number of additional shares issued as a stock dividend is so great that it has, or may be expected to have, a material effect on the market value of the stock, the transaction should be accounted for as a stock split.

In a stock split, the result is an increase in the number of shares outstanding *and* a corresponding increase (or decrease) in the par or stated value of each share. If more than 20% or 25% of the number of previously outstanding shares is to be dis-tributed, the transaction should be considered and accounted for as a stock dividend.

## ¶ 1205. Nonreciprocal Transfers with Owners

Nonreciprocal transfers between a company and its owners include:

- A distribution of nonmonetary assets (e.g., marketable equity securities) to stockholders as dividends (i.e., a dividend-in-kind).

- A distribution of nonmonetary assets (e.g., marketable equity securities) to stockholders to redeem or acquire outstanding capital stock of the company.

- A distribution of nonmonetary assets (e.g., common stock of subsidiaries or equity-method investees) to stockholders in corporate liquidations, or plans of reorganization that involve disposing of all or a significant segment of the business.

- A distribution of nonmonetary assets to groups of stockholders pursuant to plans of rescission or other settlements relating to a prior business combina-tion in order to redeem or acquire shares of stock previously issued in a busi-ness combination.

Generally, such transactions (referred to as dividends-in-kind) should be recorded at the fair value of the assets transferred, with any gain or loss recognized in current earnings.

## ¶ 1206. Treasury Stock

Treasury stock should not be reported as an asset; rather, it should be presented as a deduction from stockholders' equity. Any gain on the subsequent sale of trea-sury stock not previously retired should be credited to additional paid-in capital. Any loss on the subsequent sale should be charged to additional paid-in capital as follows:

- To the extent additional paid-in capital already includes a (net) gain from the previous sales of treasury stock.

- The remainder, if any, to retained earnings.

When a company acquires its own stock for retirement, any excess of the purchase price over the par or stated value may be allocated between additional paid-in capital and retained earnings as follows:

- To additional paid-in capital, which is limited to the amount of additional paid-in capital arising from previous retirements and (net) gains from previous sales of treasury stock of the same issue.
- The remainder, if any, to retained earnings.

Alternatively, under the retirement method, the entire amount of the excess may be charged directly to retained earnings. If the purchase price for treasury stock is less than the par value, any difference is credited entirely to additional paid-in capital.

## ¶ 1207. Quasi-Reorganizations

A quasi-reorganization is a corporate readjustment that eliminates the accumulated deficit from past unprofitable operations. As part of such a reorganization assets are restated in terms of their fair values, with the offsetting adjustment charged to retained earnings (if available) or to additional paid-in capital.

At the date of corporate readjustment, assets should be adjusted to their fair values. If the fair value of an asset cannot be determined, a conservative estimate may be made. A provision for potential losses that arise prior to the date of reorganization but for which amounts cannot be determined should be made to cover the maximum probable losses.

Any write-offs made in connection with the quasi-reorganization should be accomplished as follows:

- Write-offs to retained earnings (to the extent of a positive balance).
- Any remainder to additional paid-in capital.

Adjustments made should not be included in current earnings. If no additional paid-in capital exists or if these funds are insufficient to absorb the required changes, such capital must be created by reducing the par value of outstanding shares.

Following the quasi-reorganization, any credit balance remaining in retained earnings after giving effect to the readjustment should not be carried forward. Furthermore, the amount of additional paid-in capital created by the reorganization is restricted so that any charges against it should only be those that are properly made in connection with a newly formed entity.

IFRS

## ¶ 1208. Main Authoritative Sources

- IAS 32, *Financial Instruments: Disclosure and Presentation*

Note: IFRS does not directly (and generally) address the recognition and measurement of stockholders' equity or of its various components as separate accounting issues. Thus, following is a discussion only of selected matters.

## ¶ 1209. Warrants and Convertible Instruments

When a non-derivative financial instrument is issued, its terms should be evaluated to determine whether it contains both a liability and an equity component. A bond or similar instrument convertible by the holder into a fixed number of ordinary shares is a compound financial instrument. The economic effect of issuing such an instrument is the same as simultaneously issuing a debt instrument with an early settlement provision and warrants to purchase ordinary shares (or issuing a debt instrument with detachable share purchase warrants). First, the carrying amount of the liability component of a convertible bond must be determined by reference to the fair value of a similar liability (including any embedded non-equity derivative features) that does not have an associated equity component; the carrying amount of the equity instrument represented by the option to convert the instrument into ordinary shares is then determined by deducting the fair value of the financial liability from the fair value of the compound financial instrument as a whole.

## ¶ 1210. Redeemable Preferred Stock

Preference shares that provide for a mandatory redemption by the issuer for a fixed or determinable amount at a fixed or determinable date are considered a liability. When the initial carrying amount of redeemable preference shares is allocated to its equity and liability components, the equity component is assigned the residual amount after deducting from the fair value of the instrument as a whole the amount separately determined for the liability component.

## ¶ 1211. Stock Dividends and Splits

IFRS does not address the topic of accounting for stock dividends and stock splits.

## ¶ 1212. Nonreciprocal Transfers with Owners

IFRS does not address the topic of nonreciprocal transfers with owners (including dividends-in-kind).

## ¶ 1213. Treasury Shares

When an entity reacquires its own equity instruments (i.e., treasury shares), they should be deducted from stockholders' equity. No gain or loss should be recognized in profit or loss on the purchase, sale, issue, or cancellation of treasury shares.

## ¶ 1214. Quasi-Reorganizations

IFRS does not address the topic of quasi-reorganizations.

# ¶ 1300. Revenue

### U.S. GAAP

## ¶ 1301. Main Authoritative Sources

- SFAS No. 45, *Accounting for Franchise Fee Revenue*
- SFAS No. 48, *Revenue Recognition When Right of Return Exists*
- SFAS No. 66, *Accounting for Sales of Real Estate*
- SOP No. 81-1, *Accounting for Performance of Construction-Type and Certain Production-Type Contracts*
- SOP No. 97-2, *Software Revenue Recognition*
- SOP No. 98-9, *Modification of SOP No. 97-2, "Software Revenue Recognition," with Respect to Certain Transactions*
- EITF Issue No. 00-21, "Accounting for Revenue Arrangements with Multiple Deliverables"
- SAB No. 104, "Revenue Recognition"

Note: Generally, most guidance on revenue recognition matters relates to specific industries. While U.S. GAAP does not contain a comprehensive standard on revenue recognition, the SEC Staff, through SAB No. 104, has expressed its position regarding the application of GAAP in recognizing revenue. Although SAB No. 104 has the force of authority only on public companies, the guidance therein is also appropriate for non-SEC registrants.

## ¶ 1302. In General

In SAB No. 104, the SEC Staff clarifies that, for transactions that are within the scope of specific GAAP pronouncements, revenue should be recognized in accordance with the criteria set forth therein. Regarding a specific arrangement that is not explicitly addressed in the authoritative literature, the Staff's position is that revenue should be recognized when all of the following conditions are met:

- Persuasive evidence of an arrangement exists.
- Delivery has occurred or services have been rendered.
- The price is fixed or determinable.
- Collectibility is reasonably assured.

In the Staff's view, revenue may not be recognized until all elements of the arrangement have been finalized in accordance with the company's normal and customary policies and practices.

According to the SEC Staff, delivery is not considered to have occurred unless the customer has taken title and assumes the risks and rewards of ownership. When delivery per se has not taken place, revenue may be recognized only when the following conditions have been met:

- The customer has made a fixed commitment (preferably in writing) to purchase the goods.
- The buyer (not the seller) has requested a "bill and hold" arrangement and has a substantial business purpose for doing so.
- There is a fixed schedule for delivery that is consistent with the buyer's business purpose.
- The seller does not have any substantial additional performance requirements; the full amount of revenue may be recognized, however, when the seller has a remaining obligation for additional performance or delivery if (1) the obligation is inconsequential or perfunctory, and (2) the costs expected to be incurred upon fulfillment can be reliably estimated and they are accrued at the time the revenue is recognized.
- The seller has physically segregated the inventory and it cannot be used to fill other orders.
- The product is otherwise complete and ready for shipment.

Generally, the Staff believes that the selling price is not fixed or determinable if the customer has the unilateral right to cancel the contract and receive a full refund; revenue should not be recognized by assessing the probability that customers will not cancel contracts.

## ¶ 1303. Right of Return Exists

If a company offers the buyer the right to return the product (other than for reasons of defect under warranty provisions), revenue should be recognized at the time of sale only if all of the following conditions are met:

- The seller's price to the buyer is substantially fixed at the date of sale.
- The buyer has paid the seller or the buyer is obligated to pay the seller and the obligation is not contingent on resale of the product.
- The buyer's obligation to the seller would not be changed in the event of theft or physical destruction or damage of the product.
- The buyer acquiring the product for resale has economic substance apart from that provided by the seller.
- The seller does not have significant obligations for future performance to directly bring about resale of the product by the buyer.
- The amount of future returns can be reasonably estimated.

Sales revenue and cost of sales that are not recognized at the time of sale because all of the above conditions are not met should be recognized at the earlier of the following dates:

- When the return privilege has (substantially) expired, or
- When all of the above conditions are met.

If all of the conditions are met and the revenue is recorded, an appropriate provision for any anticipated costs or losses in connection with returns should be made.

WG&L

The ability to make a reasonable estimate of the amount of future returns depends on many factors that will vary from one case to the next; however, the following factors may impair the ability to otherwise make a reasonable estimate:

- The susceptibility of the product to significant external factors, such as technological obsolescence or changes in demand.
- The existence of relatively long periods in which a particular product may be returned.
- The absence of historical experience with similar types of sales of similar products, or the inability to apply such experience because of changing circumstances (e.g., changes in marketing policies or relationships with customers).
- The absence of a large volume of relatively homogeneous transactions.

## ¶ 1304. Franchise Revenue

Franchise fee revenue from an individual franchise sale should ordinarily be recognized (with an appropriate allowance for uncollectible amounts) when all material services or conditions relating to the sale have been substantially performed or satisfied by the franchisor; substantial performance means:

- The franchisor has no remaining obligation or intent (by agreement, trade practice, or law) to refund any cash received or forgive any unpaid amounts.
- Substantially all the initial services (e.g., site selection, training, administrative assistance) have been performed.
- No other material conditions or obligations related to the determination of any substantial performance exists.

If a large initial franchise fee is received but continuing franchise fees are insufficient to cover the cost (and a reasonable profit) of continuing services, a portion of the initial fee should be deferred and amortized over the life of the franchise. The portion deferred should be sufficient to cover estimated future costs in excess of continuing fees and to provide a reasonable profit on continuing services. Continuing franchise fees should be reported as revenue as they are earned.

## ¶ 1305. Software Revenue

If the software arrangement does not require significant production, modification, or customization, revenue should be recognized when all of the following criteria are met:

- Persuasive evidence of an arrangement exists.
- Delivery has occurred.
- Vendor's fee is fixed or determinable.
- Collectibility is probable.

For a so-called multiple element license arrangement (i.e., additional software products, upgrades, enhancements, post-contract customer support), the license fee should be allocated to the various elements based on vendor-specific objective evidence of fair value (regardless of any price that may be stated in the contract for each separate element). If sufficient vendor-specific evidence does not exist, all revenue should be deferred until (1) such evidence becomes available, or (2) all elements of the arrangement are delivered. Likewise, revenue should be deferred if a yet undelivered element is considered essential to the functionality of the delivered elements or the portion of the fee attributable to delivered elements is subject to forfeiture, refund, or other concession if the undelivered elements are not delivered.

When vendor-specific evidence of fair value exists of all undelivered elements of a multiple arrangement but such evidence is not available for one or more of the delivered elements, the residual method should be applied. Under this method, the aggregate fair value of the undelivered elements is deferred, and the difference between the total fee and the amount deferred is recognized as revenue attributable to the delivered elements.

Vendor-specific evidence of fair value is limited to the following:

- The price charged when the same element is sold separately.

- For an element not yet being sold separately, the price established by management having the relevant authority; it must be probable that the price, once established, will not change before the separate introduction of the element into the marketplace.

As for additional software to be delivered in the future pursuant to a multiple element arrangement, revenue should be allocated and recognized as follows:

- The fee allocated to an upgrade right is the price for the upgrade enhancement that would be charged to existing users of the product being upgraded (but without considering any discount that has been offered).

- The fee for additional software should be allocated among the products based on relative selling prices and recognized when all the conditions for recognition have been satisfied.

- If the software is not physically returned and the customer may continue to use such software, the arrangement should be accounted for as additional software. If the software is not physically returned and the customer may not continue to use such software, the accounting treatment depends upon whether a similar or dissimilar product is provided in exchange. If a dissimilar product is provided to the customer, the arrangement should be accounted for as a sale with a right of return; for a similar product, the transaction should be accounted for as an exchange (i.e., an actual return).

## ¶ 1306. Revenue Arrangements with Multiple Deliverables

The Emerging Issues Task Force (EITF) has reached a consensus regarding revenue arrangements with multiple deliverables. Generally, multiple deliverables involve delivery or performance of multiple products, services, or rights to use assets. Such delivery or performance (i.e., deliverables) may take place at different points in time (or over time) during the term of the arrangement. The consensus applies as follows:

- If a higher level GAAP pronouncement provides guidance concerning the determination of separate units of accounting and the method of allocating consideration to such units, the arrangement should be accounted for in accordance with that pronouncement.

- If a higher level pronouncement does not specify the manner of allocating consideration (but does provide guidance concerning the separation of deliverables within its scope), allocation should be made on a fair value basis between the deliverables within the scope of that pronouncement and those that are outside its scope. In such a case, identification of separate units of accounting (and allocation of value thereto) is governed by the provisions of the EITF consensus.

According to the consensus, revenue arrangements with multiple deliverables should be divided into separate accounting units only if the deliverables meet all of the following conditions:

- The delivered item has value to the customer on a standalone basis (i.e., the item is otherwise sold separately by any vendor or the customer could resell the item on a standalone basis).

- Objective and reliable evidence exists of the fair value of the undelivered items.

- When a customer has the general right of return on a delivered item, delivery or performance of the undelivered items must be considered probable and substantially within the vendor's control.

Revenue received by the seller should be allocated among the separate units of accounting based on their relative fair values. When there is objective and reliable evidence of the fair values of undelivered items but no such evidence exists for the items already delivered, the amount of consideration allocated to the delivered items should be computed as the remainder of the total consideration in the arrangement, less the aggregate fair value of the undelivered items.

## ¶ 1307. Real Estate Sales

A sale of real estate (other than a retail land sale) is accounted for by the full accrual method (i.e., profit is recognized in full on sale) if both:

- The amount of the profit is determinable (i.e., collectibility of the receivable is reasonably assured, or the amount that will not be collectible can be estimated).

- The earnings process is virtually complete (i.e., the seller is not obligated to perform any significant remaining activities).

Unless both conditions exist, recognition of all or part of the profit must be postponed.

To qualify for the full accrual method, all of the following criteria must be met:

- A sale is consummated.

- The buyer's initial and continuing investments are adequate to demonstrate a commitment to pay for the property.

- The seller's receivable is not subject to future subordination.

- The seller has transferred to the buyer the usual risks and rewards of ownership in a transaction that is in substance a sale and does not have a substantial continuing involvement with the property.

If all of the above criteria are not met, the sale is accounted for, depending on circumstances, under one of the following methods:

- The deposit method during construction of buildings, etc., when (1) the buyer has made a sufficient initial investment but the seller is not certain that the cost of the property will be recovered, (2) the seller guarantees a return on the investment and is uncertain as to whether the return will be realized, and (3) there is substantial certainty about the buyer's ability to make all payments.

- The cost recovery method when (1) the buyer has made a sufficient initial and continuing investment but the buyer's obligation is subordinated beyond that of a first mortgage, and (2) the transaction involves an option to purchase and the buyer has not made a sufficient initial and continuing investment.

- The reduced-profit method when the buyer has made a sufficient initial but not a sufficient continuing investment.

- The installment method when (1) there is a partial sale of real estate and collection from the buyer is not assured, (2) all the risks and rewards of ownership have not been transferred, and (3) the buyer has made a sufficient initial but not a sufficient continuing investment.

- The percentage-of-completion method when (1) the development of the project takes a period of time to complete, (2) there has already been a sale of one or more units, and (3) the buyer is committed to the purchase.

The full accrual method of accounting is applied to retail land sales if all the following conditions are met:

- Expiration of refund period. The buyer has made the down payment and each required subsequent payment until the period of cancellation with refund has expired.

- Sufficient cumulative payments. The cumulative payments of principal and interest equal or exceed 10% of the contract sales price.

- Collectibility of receivables. Collection experience for the project in which the sale is made or for the seller's prior projects indicates that at least 90% of the contracts in the project in which the sale is made that are in force six months after the sale is recorded will be collected in full; note that a down payment of at least 20% is considered to be an acceptable indication of collectibility.

- Non-subordination of receivables. The receivable from the sale is not subject to subordination to new loans on the property, except that subordination by an individual lot buyer for home construction purposes is permissible if the collection experience on those contracts is the same as on contracts not subordinated.

- Completion of development. The seller is not obligated to complete improvements of lots sold or to construct amenities or other facilities applicable to lots sold.

If all conditions for full accrual accounting are not met, retail land sales should be accounted for either under the percentage-of-completion method or the installment method.

## ¶ 1308. Long-Term Contracts

The percentage-of-completion (PC) method of accounting for long-term construction contracts is preferable if estimates of costs to complete a project and the estimated stage of completion are reasonably dependable. If they are not dependable, the completed-contract (CC) method should be used. For short-term contracts (i.e., less than one year), either method may be used because the results would be similar.

The PC method recognizes income as work on a contract progresses. The amount to be recognized in a period should be based on a method that approximately measures the progress toward completion. If current estimates of total costs indicate a loss on the contract, the entire amount of the estimated loss should be charged to operations in the period when it is discovered. Often one project consists of a number of separate but related contracts. Data on all individual contracts may be aggregated for purposes of determining the necessity of a provision for loss. During the early stages of a contract, some costs (e.g., material and subcontract) may be excluded from the determination of the amount of income to be recognized in a period if to do so would result in a more meaningful allocation of periodic income.

A modification of the PC method is the units-of-delivery method, which recognizes revenue equal to the contract price of units of a product delivered during a period. Costs allocable to the delivered units are also recognized. Costs related to undelivered units are carried in the balance sheet as inventory. The units-of-delivery method is used when an entity produces units of a basic product under production-type contracts in a continuous or sequential process to buyers' specifications.

The CC method recognizes income only when the contract is (substantially) complete. Costs and current billings are accumulated, but the only effect on operations during periods when the contract is still in progress is a charge for any estimated loss when it is discovered. As is the case when using the PC method, a provision should be made under the CC method for the amount of any expected loss on a contract at the time it is discovered.

Under the PC method, costs attributable to un-priced change orders should be treated as costs of contract performance in the period incurred if it is not probable that such costs will be recovered through a change in the contract price. If recovery is probable, such costs may either be (1) deferred until the change in contract price has been agreed upon, or (2) recorded as costs of contract performance, with revenue recognized to the extent of the costs incurred. If it is probable that the contract amount will be increased by an amount that exceeds the costs of the change order, the excess revenue should be recognized only when realization is assured beyond a reasonable doubt.

Under the CC method, costs attributable to un-priced change orders should be deferred if it is probable that they will be recovered from contract revenues. If change orders are in dispute or unapproved, they should be treated as claims. Recognition of additional revenue from claims is appropriate only if it is probable that such additional revenue will be realized and the amount is reasonably estimable; otherwise, revenue may be recognized, but only to the extent of costs incurred. Alternatively, revenues from claims may be recognized when such amounts have been received (or awarded).

IFRS

## ¶ 1309. Main Authoritative Sources

- IAS 18, *Revenue*
- IAS 11, *Construction Contracts*

## ¶ 1310. In General

Revenue is defined as the gross inflow of economic benefits during the period arising in the course of the ordinary activities of an entity when those inflows result in increases in equity, other than increases relating to contributions from equity participants. Revenue should be measured at the fair value of the consideration received or receivable.

Revenue from the sale of goods should be recognized when all the following conditions have been satisfied:

- The seller has transferred to the buyer the significant risks and rewards of ownership of the goods.

- The seller retains neither continuing managerial involvement to the degree usually associated with ownership nor effective control over the goods sold.

- The amount of revenue can be measured reliably.

- It is probable that the economic benefits associated with the transaction will flow to the entity.

- The costs incurred or to be incurred in respect of the transaction can be measured reliably.

In respect of "bill and hold" sales, in which delivery is delayed at the buyer's request but the buyer takes title and accepts billing, revenue should be recognized when the buyer takes title to the goods if the following conditions are met:

- It is probable that delivery will be made.

- The item is on hand, identified, and ready for delivery to the buyer at the time the sale is recognized. The buyer specifically acknowledges the deferred delivery instructions.
- The usual payment terms apply.

When the outcome of a transaction for the rendering of services can be estimated reliably, revenue associated with the transaction should be recognized by reference to the stage of completion of the transaction at the balance sheet date. The outcome of a transaction can be estimated reliably when all the following conditions are satisfied:

- The amount of revenue can be measured reliably.
- It is probable that the economic benefits associated with the transaction will flow to the entity.
- The stage of completion of the transaction can be measured reliably.
- The costs incurred for the transaction and the costs to complete the transaction can be measured reliably.

When the outcome of the transaction for the rendering of services cannot be estimated reliably, revenue should be recognized only to the extent of the expenses recognized that are considered recoverable.

## ¶ 1311. Right of Return Exists

If the buyer has negotiated a limited right of return, and there is uncertainty about the possibility of the return of goods, revenue should be recognized when the shipment has been formally accepted by the buyer or the goods have been delivered and the time period for rejection has elapsed.

## ¶ 1312. Franchise Revenue

The following methods of franchise fee recognition are appropriate:

- For supplies of equipment and other tangible assets, the amount of revenue should be based on the fair value of the assets sold; revenue should be recognized when the items are delivered or title passes.
- For supplies of initial and subsequent services, fees for the provision of continuing services, whether part of the initial fee or a separate fee, should be recognized as revenue as the services are rendered; when the separate fee does not cover the cost of continuing services together with a reasonable profit, part of the initial fee, sufficient to cover the costs of continuing services and to provide a reasonable profit on those services, should be deferred and recognized as revenue as the services are rendered.
- For initial services and other obligations under an area franchise arrangement, the fees attributable to the initial services should be recognized as revenue in proportion to the number of outlets for which the initial services have been substantially completed; if the initial fee is collectible over an extended period and there is a significant uncertainty that it will be collected in full, the fee should be recognized as cash installments are received.

- For continuing franchise fees, those charged for the use of continuing rights granted by the agreement or for other services provided during the period of the agreement should be recognized as revenue as the services are provided or the rights used.

- For transactions in which the franchisor is acting as an agent, no revenue should be recognized.

## ¶ 1313. Software Revenue

Fees from the development of customized software should be recognized as revenue by reference to the stage of completion of the development, including completion of services provided for post-delivery service support.

## ¶ 1314. Revenue Arrangements with Multiple Deliverables

When the selling price of a product includes an identifiable amount for subsequent servicing, an amount should be deferred to cover the expected costs of the services under the agreement, together with a reasonable profit on those services; such amount should be recognized as revenue over the period during which the service is performed.

Revenue recognition criteria should be applied to two or more transactions together when they are linked in such a way that the commercial effect cannot be understood without reference to the series of transactions as a whole.

## ¶ 1315. Real Estate Sales

Revenue on real estate sales is normally recognized when legal title passes to the buyer. In some jurisdictions, though, the equitable interest in a property may vest with the buyer before legal title passes and thus the risks and rewards of ownership have been transferred at that stage. In such cases, provided that the seller has no further substantial acts to complete under the contract, revenue may be recognized. If, however, the seller is obliged to perform any significant acts after the transfer of the equitable and/or legal title, revenue should be recognized as the acts are performed.

When real estate is sold with a degree of continuing involvement by the seller such that the risks and rewards of ownership have not been transferred, the nature and extent of the seller's continuing involvement should be the basis for determining the manner in which the transaction is accounted for. If it is accounted for as a sale, the continuing involvement of the seller may delay the recognition of revenue.

When the aggregate of the payments received by the seller (including the buyer's initial down payment and/or continuing payments by the buyer) provide insufficient evidence of the buyer's commitment to complete payment, revenue should be recognized only to the extent cash is received.

## ¶ 1316. Long-Term Contracts

When the outcome of a construction contract can be estimated reliably, contract revenue and contract costs should be recognized by reference to the stage of completion of the contract activity at the balance sheet date (i.e., the percentage-of-completion, or PC method). In certain circumstances, it may be necessary to aggregate individual contracts into a group of contracts in order to reflect the substance of a single contract or a group of contracts.

Under the PC method, contract revenue is recognized as revenue in the periods in which the work is performed, and contract costs are usually recognized as an expense in the periods in which the work to which they relate is performed. An expected loss on a contract should, however, be recognized immediately. The stage of completion of a contract may be determined in a variety of ways; the method used should reliably measure the degree of work actually performed.

When the outcome of a construction contract cannot be estimated reliably:

- Revenue should be recognized only to the extent of contract costs incurred for which recovery is probable.
- Contract costs should be recognized as an expense in the period in which they are incurred.

As is the case when using the PC method, an expected loss on the contract should be recognized immediately. The completed contract (CC) method is not permitted.

# ¶ 1400. Borrowing Costs

U.S. GAAP

## ¶ 1401. Main Authoritative Pronouncements

- SFAS No. 34, *Capitalization of Interest Cost*
- SFAS No. 58, *Capitalization of Interest Cost in Financial Statements That Include Investments Accounted for by the Equity Method*

Interest cost should be capitalized as part of the cost of constructing and acquiring certain qualified assets. Generally, the amount of interest cost to be capitalized is the actual cost of borrowings related to the qualifying assets; otherwise it is based on an allocation of interest cost incurred during the period required to complete the asset.

Interest should be capitalized on the following types of assets:

- Assets constructed or otherwise produced by a company for its own use.
- Assets constructed or produced by a third party for a company's own use for which deposits or progress payments have been made.
- Assets intended for sale or lease that are constructed or produced as discrete projects (e.g., ships or real estate developments).
- Investments (equity, loans, and advances) accounted for by the equity method made during the period of time that the investee has activities in progress necessary to begin *its* planned principal operations, *and* the investee's activities include the use of funds to acquire qualifying assets for its operations.

Interest cost should not be capitalized for the following types of assets:

- Inventory routinely manufactured in large quantities on a repetitive basis.
- Assets in use or ready for their intended use in the operations of the business.
- Assets that are not being used in the operations of the business and are not being prepared for such use.
- Assets not included in the consolidated balance sheet of the company and its subsidiaries.
- Investments accounted for by the equity method after the planned principal operations of the investee have begun.

The amount to be capitalized for qualifying assets should be that portion of the interest cost incurred during the acquisition periods that theoretically could have been avoided if expenditures for the assets had not been made. Determination of the amounts to be capitalized requires the application of an interest rate (termed the capitalization rate) to the average amount of accumulated expenditures for the particular asset during the period. The capitalization rate is based on the rate(s) applicable to the amount of outstanding debt. If a specific amount of new debt can be related to a qualifying asset, the capitalization rate used should be the interest rate on that debt. However, if the debt exceeds the expenditures for the related asset, the amount of interest to be capitalized is limited to the interest cost of the aggregate expenditures.

The total amount of interest cost to be capitalized in any period is limited to the total interest cost actually incurred in that period. (Note, however, that foreign currency gains and losses arising from borrowing funds denominated in a foreign currency may not be capitalized). In most cases, the capitalization period begins when all of the following conditions are met:

- Expenditures have been made.
- Activities necessary to prepare the qualifying asset for its intended use are under way.
- Interest cost is actually being incurred.

The interest capitalization period ends when the asset is substantially complete and ready for its intended use. If the capitalization of interest causes the overall cost of an asset to exceed its net realizable value, a provision to reduce the asset to net realizable value should be made, but interest capitalization should not be discontinued.

Interest cost not capitalized should be charged to operations as incurred during the period.

IFRS

# ¶ 1402. Main Authoritative Sources

- IAS 23, *Borrowing Costs*

Note: The following discussion is based on revised IAS 23, which becomes effective from January 1, 2009, with earlier application permitted. Under revised IAS 23, capitalization of borrowing costs is mandatory (if certain conditions are met); under prior IAS 23, which remains in effect until the mandatory effective date of revised IAS 23, borrowing costs may be charged to profit and loss as incurred (i.e., the benchmark treatment) or capitalized under specified conditions (which is referred to as the allowed alternative treatment).

Borrowing costs directly attributable to the acquisition, construction, or production of a qualifying asset form part of the cost of that asset and should be capitalized. Other borrowing costs should be recognized as an expense when incurred.

Borrowing costs may include:

- Interest on bank overdrafts and short-term and long-term borrowings.
- Amortization of discounts or premiums relating to borrowings.
- Amortization of ancillary costs incurred in connection with the arrangement of borrowings.
- Exchange differences arising from foreign currency borrowings to the extent that they are regarded as an adjustment to interest costs.

An asset qualifying for capitalization is defined as an asset that necessarily takes a substantial period of time to get ready for its intended use or sale. Inventories that are manufactured or otherwise produced over a short period of time are not qualifying assets; neither are assets that are ready for their intended use or sale when acquired.

Eligible borrowing costs include (1) those incurred during the period on funds borrowed specifically for the purpose of obtaining a qualifying asset, less any investment income on the temporary investment of those funds, and (2) the amount derived by applying the weighted average rate on general borrowings outstanding during the period (i.e., termed the capitalization rate) to expenditures on the qualifying asset. The amount capitalized during a period may not, however, exceed the amount of borrowing costs actually incurred during that period.

Capitalization of borrowing costs begins on the commencement date, which is the date on which all of the following conditions are met:

- Expenditures on the qualifying asset have been made.
- Borrowing costs are being incurred.
- Activities necessary to prepare the asset for its intended use or sale have been undertaken.

The capitalization period ceases when substantially all the activities necessary to prepare the qualifying asset for its intended use or sale are complete.

When the carrying amount or the expected ultimate cost of the qualifying asset exceeds its recoverable amount or net realizable value, the carrying amount should be written down (which write-down may be, in accordance with other IFRS, subject to subsequent reversal).

# ¶ 1500. Extraordinary, Unusual, or Infrequent Items

U.S. GAAP

## ¶ 1501. Main Authoritative Sources

- APB Opinion No. 30, *Reporting the Results of Operations—Reporting the Effects of Disposal of a Segment of a Business, and Extraordinary, Unusual, and Infrequently Occurring Events and Transactions*

To qualify as an extraordinary item, both of the following criteria must be met:

- The item must be unusual in nature (the underlying event or transaction must be abnormal and unrelated, or incidentally related, to the ordinary activities of the business); and
- The item must occur infrequently (the underlying event or transaction would not reasonably be expected to occur in the foreseeable future).

Generally, an event or transaction is presumed to be an ordinary and usual activity of the company unless the evidence clearly supports it as extraordinary and it meets both of the above criteria.

The environment in which the company operates is a primary consideration in determining whether an underlying event or transaction is unusual in nature and is not established by the fact that an event or transaction is beyond management's control. Likewise, the environment in which a company operates must be considered in determining the probability of recurrence of a specific event or transaction. As with unusual nature, the same item may be considered ordinary to one company but extraordinary to another.

The following items should *not* be reported as extraordinary because, while they are unusual in nature, they may be expected to recur in the normal course of operations:

- Write-down or write-off of receivables, inventories, equipment leased to others, or intangible assets.
- Gains or losses from exchange or translation of foreign currencies, including those relating to major devaluations and revaluations.
- Gains or losses on disposal of a component of an entity.
- Other gains or losses from the sale or abandonment of property, plant, and equipment.
- Effects of a strike, including those against competitors and major suppliers.
- Adjustment of accruals on long-term contracts.
- Costs in defense of a takeover attempt and costs incurred as part of a standstill agreement.

Even though they do not meet both criteria, the following items should be reported as extraordinary:

- The investor's share of an investee's extraordinary items.

- The net effect of discontinuing the application of SFAS No. 71, *Accounting for the Effects of Certain Types of Regulation.*
- The remaining excess of fair value of net assets acquired over cost in a business combination.

Note that the effects of virtually any significant transaction or event that is either unusual *or* infrequent (but not both) may be presented as a separate line item in the income statement, as long as it is a component of income from operations.

IFRS

## ¶ 1502. Main Authoritative Sources

- IAS 1, *Presentation of Financial Statements*

Under IFRS, no item of income or expense (or gain or loss) may be described as "extraordinary." Although no specific definitions exist of either unusual items or infrequent items, when an item of income or expense is considered material, the nature and amount of such item should be disclosed. Apart from items required to be disclosed in compliance with other IFRS, the following examples would give rise to the need for separate disclosure:

- Write-downs of inventories or property, plant, and equipment (and reversals of such write-downs).
- Disposals of property, plant, and equipment.
- Disposals of investments.
- Litigation settlements.
- Reversals of provisions.

# ¶ 1600. Discontinued Operations

## U.S. GAAP

## ¶ 1601. Main Authoritative Sources

- SFAS No. 144, *Accounting for the Impairment or Disposal of Long-Lived Assets*

A discontinued operation is defined as the sale (or the classification as held for sale) of a component of an entity. A component of an entity is the lowest level of unit at which the operations and cash flows can be clearly distinguished from the remainder of the entity. A component may be (1) a reportable segment asset, (2) a reporting unit, or (3) an asset group. A discontinued operation arises upon the disposal of a component of an entity (or upon the classification of a component as held for sale), provided that:

- The operations and cash flows of the component have been or will be eliminated from the entity's ongoing operations.
- The entity will have no significant continuing involvement in the component after disposition.

For the period in which a component has been disposed of (or classified as held for sale) and for all prior periods presented for comparative purposes, such component's results of operations should be reported as a discontinued operation. The amount reported as such (net of income tax effects) includes (1) actual operating results of the component, and (2) any gain or loss on the disposition itself, which must be separately disclosed on the face of the income statement below the caption "income from continuing operations" or in a note to the financial statements. Subsequent adjustments to a previously reported discontinued operation that are directly related to disposal of a component in a prior period should be shown as a separate element of discontinued operations.

## IFRS

## ¶ 1602. Main Authoritative Sources

- IFRS 5, *Non-Current Assets Held for Sale and Discontinued Operations*

A discontinued operation is defined as a component of an entity that either has been disposed of or is classified as held for sale and:

- Represents a separate major line of business or geographical area of operations.
- Is part of a single coordinated plan to dispose of a separate major line of business or geographical area of operations or is a subsidiary acquired exclusively with a view to resale.

A component of an entity comprises operations and cash flows that can be clearly distinguished, operationally, and for financial reporting purposes, from the remainder of the entity (i.e., a cash-generating unit or a group of cash-generating units while it was being held for use).

Discontinued operations to be reported on the face of the income statement represent a single amount comprising the total of (1) the after-tax profit or loss on the discontinued operations, plus (2) the after-tax gain or loss recognized on the write-down to fair value less costs to sell or on the disposal of the assets (or the disposal group) constituting the discontinued operations.

**WG&L**

# ¶ 1700. Taxation

## U.S. GAAP

## ¶ 1701. Main Authoritative Sources

- SFAS No. 109, *Accounting for Income Taxes*
- FASB Interpretation No. 48, *Accounting for Uncertainty in Income Taxes*

The primary objectives of accounting for income taxes are:

- Recognition of the amount of taxes payable or refundable for the current year.
- Recognition, in the form of deferred tax liabilities and assets, the future tax consequences of transactions and events that have been recognized in an enterprise's financial statements or income tax returns.

The following four basic principles are applied to achieve the primary objectives of accounting for income taxes:

- A current tax liability or asset is recognized for estimated taxes payable or refundable from tax returns prepared for the current year.
- A deferred tax liability or asset is recognized for estimated future tax effects attributable to temporary differences and carry-forwards.
- Measurement of current and deferred tax liabilities and assets is based on provisions of enacted tax law (i.e., the expected impact of future changes in the tax law or in tax rates is *not* considered).
- The gross amount of a deferred tax asset is reduced, if necessary, by the amount of tax benefits that, based on currently available evidence, are not expected to be realized.

By and large, income taxes currently payable (or refundable) for a given year result from the tax consequences of transactions and events that are recognized for financial reporting purposes in that year. However, because tax laws differ from GAAP in some important respects, differences arise between (1) the amounts of taxable and pretax financial income for a particular year and (2) the tax and financial reporting basis of assets and liabilities. These differences are referred to as "temporary" differences, because it is expected that they will result in taxable amounts (taxable temporary differences) or deductible amounts (deductible temporary differences) in future years when the related asset is recovered or the related liability is settled.

Deferred tax liabilities and assets should be determined as follows:

- Identify the types and amounts of existing temporary differences and the nature and amount of each type of operating loss and tax credit carry-forward and the remaining length of the carry-forward periods.
- Compute the total deferred tax liability for taxable temporary differences.

- Compute the total deferred tax asset for deductible temporary differences and operating loss carry-forwards.
- Reduce deferred tax assets by a valuation allowance if it is "more likely than not" (i.e., a probability of more than 50%) that some portion or all deferred tax assets will not be realized. The net amount of the deferred tax asset (i.e., after deducting the valuation allowance) should represent the amount that is more likely than not to be realized.
- Compute the deferred tax expense or benefit as the change during the year in the amount of the deferred tax liability or asset.

Note, though, that a deferred tax liability is not recognized for an excess of the amount for financial reporting purposes over the tax basis of an investment in a foreign subsidiary or in a foreign corporate joint venture if evidence shows that the foreign subsidiary or joint venture has invested (or will invest) the undistributed earnings indefinitely or that such earnings will be remitted in a tax-free liquidation.

A deferred tax liability or asset should be measured using the enacted tax rate expected to apply to taxable income in the periods in which the liability will be settled or the asset recovered. If graduated tax rates are a significant factor, a deferred tax liability or asset should be measured using the average graduated tax rate applicable to the amount of estimated annual taxable income in the periods in which the deferred amount is expected to reverse.

Deferred tax liabilities and assets should be adjusted for the effects of a change in tax laws or rates. Thus, a deferred tax asset or liability that was recognized at an enacted rate expected to be in effect when the asset is realized or the liability is settled should be increased or decreased to reflect newly enacted rates that will be in effect in the years of reversal. The amount of the adjustment should be included in income tax expense or benefit for the year that includes the enactment date.

Income tax expense for an interim period should be allocated among:

- Continuing operations.
- Discontinued operations.
- Extraordinary items.
- Other comprehensive income.
- Items charged or credited directly to equity.

If only one element of net income other than continuing operations is present, the portion remaining after allocation to continuing operations is attributed to that element. If there are two or more additional elements of net income, the remaining amount should be allocated among them in proportion to their individual effects on income tax expense or benefit.

The financial statement effects of a tax position should be recognized when it is more likely than not that such position, based on its technical merits, will be sustained upon examination (including resolution of appeals or litigation) by the taxing authorities. In assessing the more-likely-than-not criterion, the entity should (1) assume that the tax position will be examined by the applicable taxing authority having full knowledge of all relevant information, and (2) evaluate each position without consideration of the possibility of offset or aggregation of other positions.

A recognized tax position should be initially and subsequently measured at the largest amount of the benefit that carries a greater than 50% likelihood of being realized upon settlement. In determining the amount to be recognized, consideration should be given to the probabilities of various outcomes using the facts and circumstances available at the entity's reporting date. A recognized tax position should be derecognized in the first period in which it is no longer more likely than not that the position would be sustained upon examination. Note that the use of a valuation allowance is not permitted as a substitute for derecognition.

IFRS

# ¶ 1702. Main Authoritative Sources

- IAS 12, *Income Taxes*

Current tax payable should be recognized as a liability; if the amount already paid for the current and prior periods exceeds the amount due for such periods, the excess should be recognized as an asset. A deferred tax liability should be recognized for taxable temporary differences. A deferred tax asset should be recognized for all deductible temporary differences to the extent that it is probable that taxable profit will be available against which the deductible temporary difference can be utilized.

Temporary differences are differences between the carrying amount of an asset or liability in the balance sheet and its tax base. Temporary differences may be either:

- Taxable temporary differences: temporary differences that will result in taxable amounts in determining taxable profit or loss of future periods when the carrying amount of the asset or liability is recovered or settled.

- Deductible temporary differences: temporary differences that will result in amounts that are deductible in determining taxable profit or loss of future periods when the carrying amount of the asset or liability is recovered or settled.

Deferred tax assets and liabilities should be measured at the tax rates expected to apply to the period when the asset is realized or the liability is settled, based on tax rates (and tax laws) that have been enacted or substantively enacted at the balance sheet date (and should not be discounted). The carrying amount of a deferred tax asset should be reviewed at each balance sheet date, and, if applicable, reduced to the extent it is no longer probable that sufficient taxable profit will be available to allow the benefit of part or all of that deferred tax asset to be utilized. Any such reduction should be reversed to the extent that it becomes probable that sufficient taxable profit will be available.

Current and deferred tax expense (or benefit) should be included in profit or loss for the period, except that it should be charged or credited directly to equity if the tax relates to items that are, themselves, credited or charged directly to equity in the same or a different period.

A deferred tax liability should be recognized for all taxable temporary differences associated with investments in subsidiaries, branches and associates, and interests in joint ventures, except to the extent that (1) the parent, investor, or venturer is able to control the timing of the reversal of the temporary difference, and (2) it is probable that the temporary difference will not reverse in the foreseeable future. A deferred tax asset for all deductible temporary differences arising from investments in subsidiaries, branches and associates, and interests in joint ventures should also be recognized, except to the extent that it is probable the temporary difference will reverse in the foreseeable future, and taxable profit will be available against which the temporary difference can be utilized.

# ¶ 1800. Earnings Per Share

### U.S. GAAP

## ¶ 1801. Main Authoritative Sources

- SFAS No. 128, *Earnings per Share*

Basic earnings per share (EPS) is computed simply by dividing income available to common stockholders by the weighted average number of common shares actually outstanding during the period. Income available to common stockholders is determined after deducting preferred dividends declared plus dividends accumulated (to the extent earned) for the period on cumulative preferred stock. For purposes of basic EPS, the weighted average number of shares outstanding for the period includes contingently issuable shares (i.e., shares issuable for little or no cash consideration upon the satisfaction of the conditions of a contingent stock agreement) as of the date that all necessary conditions have been met.

Diluted EPS presents, on a per share basis, income attributable to common shares actually outstanding plus dilutive potential common shares outstanding during the period. Such potential common shares include options and warrants, convertible debt, and convertible preferred stock.

In general, the effects of options and warrants on diluted EPS are reflected through application of the treasury stock method, whereby the proceeds received by the entity based on assumed exercise are hypothetically used to repurchase the entity's common stock at the average market price for the period. Dilution will occur pursuant to the treasury stock method only if the average market price of the entity's common stock is higher than the exercise price of the related options and warrants (i.e., they are "in the money"). When the opposite is present (i.e., the average market price is lower), the results will be antidilutive, and thus the impact of options and warrants are ignored.

The effects of securities convertible into common stock are reflected in diluted EPS using the if-converted method, which requires adjustments for:

- Preferred dividends that would not have been declared if convertible preferred stock were converted.

- Interest on convertible debt (net of tax effect) that would not have been accrued if the convertible debt were converted.

- Nondiscretionary (e.g., profit sharing, royalty) expenses or charges (net of tax effect) that would have been computed differently had the interest on convertible debt not been recognized.

- The incremental common stock that would have been issued upon assumed conversion of preferred stock and debt.

Convertible preferred stock and debt should be assumed converted only when their effects are dilutive.

Shares that are contingently issuable upon the satisfaction of certain conditions should be included in diluted EPS as of the beginning of the period in which the specified conditions were met. If the condition to be met is attainment or maintenance of earnings, the additional shares to be issued should be included in diluted EPS based on the assumption that the current amount of earnings will remain unchanged until the end of the agreement. If the specified condition involves the future market price of the stock, diluted EPS should reflect the number of additional shares to be issued based on the market price at the end of the reporting period. When both future earnings and future market prices must be met, diluted EPS should be based on both conditions at the end of the reporting period; if, however, either condition is not satisfied at the end of the reporting period, no additional shares should be included in the computation of diluted EPS. If the contingency is not based on earnings or market price, diluted EPS should include the number of additional shares to be issued based on the assumption that the present status of the condition will remain unchanged until the end of the contingency period.

If an entity issues a contract that may be settled either in common stock or cash (e.g., a written put option that gives the holder the choice of obtaining settlement in stock or in cash), it should be presumed that the contract will be settled in stock (and thus the shares to be issued should be added to the denominator in the computation of diluted EPS). This also applies to share-based compensation arrangements payable in stock or cash at the option of either the entity or the employee.

In some capital structures, participating securities and/or two classes of common stock are present. A participating security participates in dividends with common stock pursuant to a predetermined formula. For nonconvertible securities, the two-class method should be used in computing EPS, as follows:

- Net income from continuing operations is reduced by the amount of dividends declared in the current period for each class of stock and by the contractual amount of dividends (or interest on participating income bonds) that must be paid for the current period (e.g., unpaid cumulative dividends).

- The remaining earnings are allocated to common stock and participating securities to the extent that each security is entitled to share in earnings as if all the earnings for the period had been distributed.

- Total earnings allocated to each security is divided by the number of outstanding shares of that security.

Basic and diluted EPS should be retroactively adjusted for the effects of stock dividends or stock splits (including reverse splits). If either of these take place after the end of the period but before the financial statements are issued, per share amounts for the latest period and any prior periods presented for comparative purposes should be based on the new number of shares.

In connection with a rights issue to existing shareholders, the discount from market value is deemed similar to a stock dividend. Accordingly, both basic and diluted EPS should be retroactively adjusted for all periods presented giving effect to the discount.

Entities with simple capital structures (i.e., those with only common stock and no potential common stock) are required to present on the face of the income statement basic EPS for income from continuing operations (or as applicable, for the caption describing income before extraordinary items and/or the cumulative effect of an accounting change) and for net income, separately for each class of common stock outstanding. Entities having both common stock and potential common stock must present on the face of the income statement basic and diluted EPS for the same captions by each class of common stock.

IFRS

## ¶ 1802. Main Authoritative Sources

- IAS 33, *Earnings per Share*

Basic earnings per share (EPS) is calculated by dividing profit or loss attributable to ordinary equity holders of the parent entity (the numerator) by the weighted average number of ordinary shares outstanding (the denominator) during the period. Amounts attributable to ordinary equity holders of the parent entity are determined by deducting from profit and loss of the parent after-tax amounts of preference dividends on non-cumulative preference shares declared for the period and dividends for cumulative preference shares required for the period, whether or not the dividends have been declared. Contingently issuable shares should be treated as outstanding and included in the calculation of basic EPS only from the date when all necessary conditions are satisfied.

Diluted EPS presents profit or loss attributable to ordinary equity holders of the parent entity based on the weighted average number of shares outstanding, adjusted for the effects of all dilutive potential ordinary shares. Potential ordinary shares should be treated as dilutive when their conversion to ordinary shares would decrease earnings per share or increase loss per share from continuing operations.

For the purpose of calculating diluted EPS, the exercise of dilutive options and warrants should be assumed, with the assumed proceeds having been received from the issuance of ordinary shares at the average market price of such shares during the period. The difference between the number of ordinary shares issued and the number of ordinary shares that would have been issued at the average market price of ordinary shares during the period should be treated as an issue of ordinary shares for no consideration.

In the computation of diluted EPS, the dilutive effect of convertible instruments should give effect to (1) dividends on convertible preferred stock and interest on convertible debt that would not have been paid upon assumed conversion, and (2) the number of ordinary shares that would have been issued.

If attainment or maintenance of a specified amount of earnings is the condition for contingent issue and if that amount has been attained at the end of the reporting period (and it must be maintained beyond the current period), the additional ordinary shares should be treated as outstanding (if the effect is dilutive) for purposes of computing diluted EPS. If the number of ordinary shares contingently issuable depends on the future market price of the ordinary shares, the calculation of diluted

EPS should be based on the number of ordinary shares that would be issued if the market price at the end of the current period were the market price at the end of the contingency period. If the condition is based on an average of market prices over a period of time that extends beyond the end of the current period, the average for the time period that has lapsed should be used.

If the number of ordinary shares contingently issuable depends on future earnings and future prices of the ordinary shares, the number of ordinary shares included in diluted EPS should be based on both conditions (i.e., earnings to date and the current market price at the end of the current period). Contingently issuable ordinary shares should not be included in the diluted EPS calculation unless both conditions are met.

If the number of ordinary shares contingently issuable depends on a condition other than earnings or market price, the assumption should be made that the present status of the condition will remain unchanged until the end of the contingency period.

If an entity has issued a contract that may be settled in ordinary shares or cash at the entity's option, it should be presumed that the contract will be settled in ordinary shares, and the resulting potential ordinary shares should be included in the computation diluted EPS.

When there is more than one class of ordinary shares, earnings should be apportioned to the different classes of shares in accordance with their dividend rights or other rights of participation.

The weighted average number of ordinary shares outstanding during the period and for all periods presented should be adjusted for events, other than the conversion of potential ordinary shares that have changed the number of ordinary shares outstanding without a corresponding change in resources. Examples include:

- A capitalization or bonus issue (sometimes referred to as a stock dividend).
- A bonus element in any other issue (e.g., a bonus element in a rights issue to existing shareholders).
- A share split (or reverse share split).

# ¶ 1900. Accounting Changes
## U.S. GAAP

## ¶ 1901. Main Authoritative Sources
- SFAS No. 154, *Accounting Changes and Error Corrections*

## ¶ 1902. Accounting Changes

A change in accounting principle is defined as a change from one generally accepted accounting principle to another generally accepted accounting principle when there are two or more such principles that apply or when the accounting principle formerly used is no longer generally accepted. All changes in accounting principle must be accounted for retrospectively (i.e., retroactively), unless it is impracticable to determine either (1) the period-specific effects or (2) the cumulative effect of the change. A change in accounting principle is permitted only if a change is required by a newly issued accounting pronouncement or the new principle can be justified on the basis of its preferability.

Upon retrospective application:

- The cumulative effect of the change to the new principle is reflected in the carrying amounts of assets and liabilities as of the beginning of the first period for which financial statements are presented.
- Any offsetting adjustment is made to the opening balance in retained earnings of the first period presented.
- Financial statements for each individual prior period presented are adjusted to reflect the period-specific effects of applying the new principle.

If the cumulative effect can be determined but it is impracticable to determine the period-specific effects on all periods presented, the cumulative effect of the change should be applied to the carrying amounts of assets and liabilities as of the beginning of the earliest period to which the new principle can be applied, with any offsetting adjustment made to opening retained earnings for that period. If it is impracticable to determine the cumulative effect of the change on any prior period, the change should be applied prospectively as of the earliest practicable date.

Retrospective application should include only the direct (including income tax) effects of the change. Indirect effects that would have been recognized if the new principle had been followed in earlier periods (e.g., nondiscretionary expenses) should not be included in the retrospective application. Indirect effects actually incurred and recognized, however, should be reported in the period in which the change is made.

A change in accounting estimate should be accounted for in (1) the period of change if the change affects that period only, or (2) the period of change and future periods if the change affects both. Note that a change in accounting estimate may not be accounted for by restating or retrospectively adjusting amounts reported in financial statements of prior periods or by reporting pro forma amounts for prior periods.

## ¶ 1903. Error Corrections

An error in previously issued financial statements is an error in recognition, measurement, presentation, or disclosure in financial statements resulting from mathematical mistakes, mistakes in the application of GAAP, or oversight or misuse of facts that existed at the time the financial statements were prepared (including a change from an accounting principle that is not generally accepted to one that is).

An error in the financial statements of a prior period discovered subsequent to the issuance of such statements should be accounted for as a prior-period adjustment by retrospectively restating the prior period financial statements, as follows:

- The cumulative effect of the error on periods prior to those presented should be reflected in the carrying amounts of assets and liabilities as of the beginning of the first period presented.
- An offsetting adjustment should be made to the opening balance of retained earnings for that period.
- Financial statements for each individual prior period presented should be adjusted to reflect correction of the period-specific effects of the error.

IFRS

## ¶ 1904. Main Authoritative Sources

- IAS 8, *Accounting Policies, Changes in Accounting Estimates and Errors*

## ¶ 1905. Accounting Changes

A change in accounting policy (not mandated by a specific standard or interpretation) may be made only if it results in reliable and more relevant information regarding the entity's financial position, financial performance, or cash flows.

All voluntary changes in accounting policy must be accounted for retrospectively (i.e., as if the new policy had always been applied) unless it is impracticable to determine either the period-specific effects or the cumulative effect of the change. Retrospective application requires adjustment of the opening balance of retained earnings and of affected individual affected assets and liabilities for the earliest period presented.

When it is impracticable to determine the period-specific effects of changing an accounting policy for one or more prior periods presented, the new accounting policy should be applied to the carrying amounts of assets and liabilities as at the beginning of the earliest period for which retrospective application is practicable, with a corresponding adjustment to the opening balance of each affected component of equity for that period. When it is impracticable to determine the cumulative effect of applying a new accounting policy to all prior periods, the new policy should be accounted for prospectively from the earliest date practicable.

The effect of a change in accounting estimate should be accounted for in (1) the period of the change if the change affects that period only, or (2) the period of the change and future periods if the change affects both.

WG&L

## ¶ 1906. Error Corrections

Prior period errors are defined as omissions from and misstatements in financial statements for one or more prior periods arising from a failure to use (or misuse of) reliable information that (1) was available when the financial statements for those periods were authorized for issuance, and (2) could reasonably be expected to have been obtained and taken into account in the preparation and presentation of those financial statements. Errors include the effects of mathematical mistakes, mistakes in applying accounting policies, oversights, or misinterpretations of facts, and fraud.

A subsequently discovered error should be corrected retrospectively in the first set of financial statements authorized for issues after their discovery by (1) restating the comparative amounts for all prior periods presented in which the error occurred, or (2) restating the opening balances of assets, liabilities, and equity for the earliest prior period presented if the error occurred before such period.

If it is impracticable to determine the period-specific effects or the cumulative effect of the error, it should be accounted for in the same manner as a change in accounting policy for which it is impossible to determine the effects.

# ¶ 2000. Accounting Policies

U.S. GAAP

## ¶ 2001. Main Authoritative Sources

- APB Opinion No. 22, *Disclosure of Accounting Policies*

Accounting policies are the specific principles and methods that a company considers to be the most appropriate in the circumstances to present fairly its financial statements in conformity with GAAP. Generally, disclosure should relate to:

- A choice from one of existing acceptable alternatives.
- Principles and methods peculiar to the industry in which the company operates, even if those principles and methods are predominantly followed in that industry.
- Unusual or innovative applications of GAAP.

The foregoing specific requirements notwithstanding, the overriding theme is that all accounting principles materially affecting the determination of financial position, results of operations, or cash flows should be identified and described.

IFRS

## ¶ 2002. Main Authoritative Sources

- IAS 8, *Accounting Policies, Changes in Accounting Estimates and Errors*

Disclosure of accounting policies should include the measurement basis (or bases) used in preparing the financial statements and other accounting policies applied that are relevant to an understanding of the financial statements. In addition, disclosure should be made of the judgments (apart from those involving estimates) that management has made in the process of applying the entity's accounting policies and that have the most significant effect on the amounts recognized in the financial statements.

In selecting an accounting policy for a transaction or event for which an IFRS standard or IRIC interpretation does not specify treatment, consideration should be given to (1) requirements and guidance contained in standards and interpretations covering similar or related issues, (2) definitions, recognition criteria, and measurement concepts contained in the IFRS conceptual framework, (3) the most recent pronouncements of other standard setters that use a similar conceptual framework for developing accounting standards, and (4) other accounting literature and industry practice.

# ¶ 2100. Business Combinations

## U.S. GAAP

## ¶ 2101. Main Authoritative Sources

- SFAS No. 141, *Business Combinations*

**Note:** In December 2007, the FASB issued SFAS No. 141(R), which becomes effective for fiscal years beginning on or after December 15, 2008 (i.e., the 2009 calendar year); early application of SFAS No. 141(R) is *not* permitted. The discussion in this section is based on SFAS No. 141, which remains applicable until the effective date of SFAS No. 141(R); it is followed by a summary of the major changes in accounting for business combinations in SFAS No. 141(R).

Only the purchase method may be applied to account for a business combination that is deemed to be the acquisition of one company (or more than one company) by another. As such, the acquiring company records the net assets (assets acquired less liabilities assumed) at its cost. Results of operations of the acquiring company include the operations of the acquired company only from the date of acquisition. A business combination is defined as the acquisition of (1) net assets that constitute a business, or (2) equity interests in an entity (or more than one entity) that results in control by the acquirer over that entity. Note, though, that, in an exchange of shares or transfer of assets between companies under common control, the net assets or equity interests received should be recognized at the carrying amounts as of the date of transfer.

Generally, the acquirer is the entity disbursing cash, distributing other assets, or assuming liabilities. Typically (but not always), the acquirer is the larger entity. In determining which entity should be deemed the acquirer, the following matters should be considered:

- Relative voting rights of the combined entity. Usually, the acquirer is the entity whose owners retain or receive the largest share of such rights.

- Existence of a large minority voting interest. When no other owner (or organized group of owners) holds a significant voting interest, the acquirer is the entity whose owners hold the largest minority voting interest in the combined entity.

- Composition of the governing body. Generally, the acquirer is the entity whose owners (or governing body) have the authority to elect or appoint a voting majority of the board of directors (or its equivalent) in the combined entity.

- Composition of senior management. In most cases, the acquirer is the entity whose senior management (i.e., chairman, CEO, president, and CFO and divisional heads reporting to such officers) dominates the combined entity.

- Terms of exchange of equity securities. When equity securities of publicly traded companies are exchanged, the acquirer is the entity paying a premium over the market price of the securities of the other entity.

When more than two entities are involved in a business combination, the acquirer may be (1) the entity initiating the combination, or (2) the entity whose assets, revenues, and earning substantially exceed those of the others. If a new entity is created to absorb the constituent entities to a business combination, all of the foregoing factors should be evaluated in determining the identity of the acquiring company. When a purchase is accomplished upon the formation of a new company whose shares are being exchanged for the outstanding shares of each of the combining entities, the entity whose former shareholders either retain or receive the larger portion of the voting stock of the combined company should ordinarily be considered the acquirer.

Ordinarily, the date of an acquisition is the date on which the consideration for the purchase is distributed. For convenience, though, the end of an accounting period falling between the initiation date and the consummation date may be designated the effective date of the purchase.

Cost of the acquisition is determined on the basis of the fair value of the consideration given (which includes direct and out-of-pocket costs) or of the net assets or stock received, whichever is more reliable and readily determinable. When based on future earnings (or other operating) levels of the acquired company, the value of the additional consideration when ultimately paid should be added to the original cost of the acquisition. When based on future market price, the fair value of the additional (contingent) consideration ultimately issued should be added to the original cost of the acquisition. When contingent consideration is based in part on future earnings levels and in part on future market price, the amount of contingent consideration should be separated into its respective elements and each accounted for individually.

Whether net assets or common stock is acquired, fair values of the assets and liabilities of the acquired company must be assigned, including the fair values of pre-acquisition contingencies. At the date of acquisition, an intangible asset (apart from goodwill) should be recognized if it arises from contractual or other legal rights (even if such rights are transferable or separable from the acquired entity or from other rights and obligations). An intangible asset not arising from contractual or legal rights should be recorded only if it is capable of being separated from the acquiring entity and thus can be sold, transferred, licensed, rented, or exchanged on its own (whether or not there is an intention of doing so). Allocation of the purchase price should be made to R&D of the acquired entity, including capitalized costs resulting from R&D activities or to be used in such activities by the combined enterprise. However, costs to be used for a particular R&D project that have no alternative future use should be charged to operations at the date of the purchase.

Goodwill represents the remainder of the cost of an acquired entity over the net amounts assigned to assets acquired (including intangibles) and liabilities assumed. Goodwill should be recognized as an asset as of the date of acquisition. When the sum of amounts assigned to assets and liabilities exceeds the cost of the acquired entity (so-called negative goodwill), that excess should first be allocated as a pro rata reduction of the amounts assigned to all assets acquired, except for the following:

- Financial assets.
- Assets to be disposed of by sale.
- Deferred tax assets.
- Prepaid assets relating to pension or other postretirement benefits.
- Other current assets.

If, upon reducing all qualifying assets acquired to zero balances, any excess remains, it should be reported in the income statement as an extraordinary gain for the period in which the business combination is completed.

## ¶ 2102. Major Changes in SFAS No. 141(R)

SFAS No. 141(R) retains the fundamental requirements of its predecessor that the purchase method be applied to all business combinations; note that, in SFAS No. 141(R), the purchase method is referred to as the acquisition method. Major changes from the previous standard include the following:

- The date on which the acquirer obtains control of the acquiree has been definitively established as the acquisition date.
- While SFAS No. 141 provides guidance for identifying the acquirer, it does not explicitly define the acquirer; SFAS No. 141(R) defines the acquirer in a business combination as the entity that obtains control of the acquiree.
- SFAS No. 141(R), with limited exceptions, requires assets acquired and liabilities assumed to be recognized at their fair values; that requirement replaces the so-called cost-allocation process in SFAS No. 141, under which the cost of an acquisition is allocated to individual assets and liabilities based on estimated fair values.
- Whereas, pursuant to SFAS No. 141, costs incurred to effect the business combination are included in the allocated cost, SFAS No. 141(R) requires acquisition-related costs to be recognized separately from the acquisition.
- SFAS No. 141 does not provide guidance in respect of the measurement of the noncontrolling interest (previously referred to as the minority interest) at the date of acquisition; SFAS 141(R) requires the noncontrolling interest to be measured at fair value.
- Pursuant to SFAS No. 141, goodwill recognized on the date of acquisition represents only the amount attributable to the acquirer; under SFAS No. 141(R), because the noncontrolling (i.e., minority) interest is measured at fair value, the amount of goodwill recognized is attributable to both the acquirer and the noncontrolling interest.
- Under SFAS No. 141, contingent consideration obligations are recognized when the contingency is resolved and the consideration is issued or becomes issuable; under SFAS No. 141(R), contingent consideration is recognized (as part of the aggregate consideration transferred in the transaction) on the date of acquisition and measured at fair value.
- SFAS No. 141 requires so-called negative goodwill to be allocated pro rata to amounts that otherwise would be assigned to specific assets acquired (with

the remainder after such allocation reported as an extraordinary gain); SFAS No. 141(R) requires that the entire excess of the acquisition-date fair value of identifiable net assets acquired over the fair value of consideration transferred plus, if applicable, the acquisition-date fair value of the noncontrolling interest be recognized as a gain.

IFRS

## ¶ 2103. Main Authoritative Sources

- IFRS 3, *Business Combinations*
- IAS 38, *Intangible Assets*

**Note:** In January 2008, the IASB issued revised IFRS 3, which becomes effective for fiscal years beginning on or after July 1, 2009, with early application permitted. The discussion in this section is based on IFRS 3, which remains applicable until the mandatory effective date of revised IFRS 3; it is followed by a summary of the major changes in accounting for business combinations in revised IFRS 3.

A business combination is defined as the bringing together of separate entities or businesses into one reporting entity. All business combinations must be accounted for by applying the purchase method. Upon consummation of a business combination, the acquiring company records the net assets at its cost and results of operations of the acquiring company include the operations of the acquired company only from the date of acquisition. Accounting for a business combination involving entities or businesses under common control is not addressed.

The acquirer in a business combination is the combining entity that obtains control of the other combining entities or businesses. Generally, control of the acquirer is obtained over the acquired company when the acquired company obtains the power:

- Over more than 50% of the voting rights of the other entity by virtue of an agreement with other investors.
- To govern the financial and operating policies of the other entity under a statute or an agreement.
- To appoint or remove the majority of the members of the board of directors or equivalent governing body of the other entity.
- To cast the majority of votes at meetings of the board of directors or equivalent governing body of the other entity.

When a business combination involves more than two combining entities, one of the combining entities that existed before the combination should be identified as the acquirer. Determining the acquirer in such cases should include consideration of, among other factors, (1) which of the combining entities initiated the combination, and (2) whether the assets or revenues of one of the combining entities significantly exceed those of the others. In a business combination effected through an exchange of equity interests, the entity that issues the equity interests is normally deemed the acquirer.

Normally, in a single transaction, the date of acquisition is the date on which the acquirer effectively obtains control of the acquiree.

Cost of a business combination is the sum of (1) the fair values, at the date of exchange, of assets given, liabilities incurred or assumed, and equity instruments issued by the acquirer, in exchange for control of the acquiree, plus (2) any costs directly attributable to the business combination. When an acquisition provides for an adjustment to the cost of the combination contingent on future events, the amount of the adjustment should be included in the cost of the combination at the acquisition date (or at a later date) if (when) the adjustment is probable and can be measured reliably.

The cost of the business combination must be allocated to assets acquired and liabilities assumed (including contingencies that can be measured reliably) at their respective fair values. At the date of acquisition, an intangible asset, which includes acquired in-process research and development, should be recognized if its fair value can be reliably measured and (1) it is separable (i.e., capable of being separated or divided and sold, transferred, licensed, rented or exchanged, either individually or together with a related contract, asset or liability), or (2) it arises from contractual or other legal rights, regardless of whether those rights are transferable or separable from the entity or from other rights and obligations.

Goodwill represents the excess of the cost of the business combination over the acquirer's interest in the net fair value of the recognized identifiable assets and liabilities. If the acquirer's interest in the net fair value of recognized identifiable assets and liabilities exceeds the cost of the business combination, the acquirer should (1) reassess the identification and measurement of such assets and liabilities and the measurement of the cost of the business combination, and (2) immediately recognize any remaining excess in profit or loss.

## ¶ 2104. Major Changes in Revised IFRS 3

Revised IFRS 3 retains the fundamental requirements of its predecessor that the purchase method be applied to all business combinations; note that the purchase method is now referred to as the acquisition method. Major changes from the previous standard include the following:

- All acquisition-related costs incurred are now required to be treated as period costs (rather than capitalized as part of the cost of the acquisition).

- The noncontrolling interest (previously referred to as the minority interest) at the date of acquisition may be measured either at (1) fair value, or (2) the noncontrolling interest's proportionate share of the net identifiable assets of the acquired entity.

- Goodwill at the acquisition date is measured as the difference between the aggregate of (1) the fair value of the consideration transferred plus the amount of any noncontrolling interest in the acquired entity, and (2) the net amount of identifiable assets acquired less liabilities assumed.

Contingent consideration obligations must be measured at fair value as of the acquisition date and recognized as part of the aggregate consideration transferred in the transaction.

# ¶ 2200. Consolidated and Combined Statements

U.S. GAAP

## ¶ 2201. Main Authoritative Sources

- ARB No. 51, *Consolidated Financial Statements*
- SFAS No. 140, *Accounting for Transfers and Servicing of Financial Assets and Extinguishments of Liabilities*
- FASB Interpretation No. 46(R), *Consolidation of Variable Interest Entities*

## ¶ 2202. Consolidated Statements in General

Consolidated financial statements are presumed to be more meaningful than separate statements and are usually necessary for a fair presentation when one company has direct (or indirect) control over one or more other companies. The effect of consolidated statements is to present financial position, results of operations, and cash flows of a parent company and its subsidiaries as if the group were a single entity. As a general rule, direct (or indirect) ownership of more than 50% of the outstanding voting stock of a company is a condition that ordinarily points to consolidation. The only exception to this general rule is when control does not rest with the majority owners (e.g., a subsidiary is in reorganization or bankruptcy).

A difference in fiscal years of a parent and a subsidiary does not justify the exclusion of the subsidiary from consolidation. When the difference is not more than three months, it is acceptable to use the subsidiary's statements for purposes of consolidation with its parent. When the difference is more than three months, statements for the subsidiary should be prepared that approach the parent's fiscal year (i.e., not more than three months apart).

Minority interest is presented in the consolidated balance sheet at an amount equal to the minority ownership percentage of the book value of the subsidiary's net assets. The minority interest in the consolidated income statement is equal to the minority ownership percentage of the subsidiary's recognized net income or loss. Both amounts are based on amounts after elimination of intercompany profits or losses. The amount of goodwill in the consolidated balance sheet is equal to the excess of the parent's purchase price over the fair value of the net assets acquired. The fair value increment of the acquired subsidiary's net assets on the consolidated balance sheet is limited to the amount attributable to the parent's ownership percentage.

Significant intercompany transactions and balances should be eliminated in consolidation. Even if there is a minority interest, 100% of any intercompany profits (or losses) remaining at the date of the financial statements should be eliminated, and it should be allocated proportionately between the parent and the minority interest.

**Note:** In December 2007, the FASB issued SFAS No. 160, *Noncontrolling Interests in Consolidated Financial Statements*, which amends ARB No. 51. SFAS No. 160 becomes effective for fiscal years beginning on or after December 15, 2008, with early application prohibited. Following are the principal changes made to ARB No. 51 by SFAS No. 160.

- It clarifies that a noncontrolling interest (previously referred to as a minority interest) represents an ownership interest in the consolidated entity that should be reported as equity in the consolidated financial statements (rather than, as was previously the case, as a liability or in the mezzanine section of the balance sheet between liabilities and equity).

- It requires consolidated net income to be reported at an amount that includes the amount attributable to the parent and the amount attributable to the noncontrolling interest (rather than, as was previously the case, as an expense or other deduction in arriving at consolidated net income).

- It requires expanded financial statement presentation and disclosures that clearly identify and distinguish the interests of the parent company's owners and those of the noncontrolling interest in a subsidiary.

## ¶ 2203. Combined Statements

In order to prepare consolidated statements, a controlling interest (more than 50%) must rest directly or indirectly with one member of the consolidated group. There are circumstances, however, under which combined (as distinguished from consolidated) statements of commonly controlled enterprises are more meaningful than separate statements. Examples of such circumstances are:

- A controlling interest in several companies that are related in their operations rests with one individual or company.

- Several companies operate under common management.

- A group of unconsolidated subsidiaries have their financial position and results of operations presented together.

When combined statements are prepared, intercompany transactions and gains or losses should be eliminated, and any minority interest in one or more of the companies as well as other matters that ordinarily pertain to the consolidation of subsidiaries with their parent should be accounted for in the same manner as in consolidated statements.

## ¶ 2204. Variable Interest Entities

A variable interest in an entity is an interest that changes as changes occur in that entity's net asset value. An enterprise that absorbs a majority of an entity's expected losses and receives a majority of its expected residual returns resulting from one or more variable interests in a variable interest entity (VIE) is termed the primary beneficiary. The financial statements of a VIE must be consolidated into those of its primary beneficiary. Types of variable interests include the following:

- Equity investments to the extent that they are at risk.

- Guarantees of the values of assets or liabilities (including written put options) that protect holders of senior interests from losses.

- Forward contracts to purchase assets or equity interests from a VIE or to sell assets or issue equity securities to a VIE.

- Held or written swaps (particularly total return swaps and similar arrangements) that transfer substantially all the risk and returns related to certain assets without actually transferring the assets themselves.

- Service contracts (if compensation is designed to be significantly different from the market value of the services performed).

In determining whether an enterprise is a primary beneficiary, its rights and obligations conveyed by the enterprise's variable interests should be taken into account (including the relationship of such variable interests with those held by others); if the enterprise's variable interests will absorb a majority of the VIE's expected losses and/or receive a majority of its expected residual returns, the enterprise is the primary beneficiary, and it should consolidate the VIE. If one enterprise will absorb a majority of the VIE's losses but another enterprise will receive a majority of its expected residual returns, the enterprise absorbing the losses should consolidate the VIE. Expected losses represent expected negative variability in the fair value of the entity's net assets, exclusive of variable interests; expected residual returns represent the expected positive variability in the fair value of its net assets, exclusive of variable interests.

Determination of an enterprise's status as a primary beneficiary should be made at the time of initial involvement. Reconsideration is required (1) if the VIE's governing documents or contractual arrangements are subsequently modified in a way that reallocates between the existing primary beneficiary and other related parties the obligation to absorb the VIE's expected losses or the right to receive its expected residual returns, or (2) when the primary beneficiary sells or otherwise disposes of all or part of its variable interest to unrelated parties. A holder of a variable interest that is not the primary beneficiary also must reconsider its status if it acquires newly issued interests in the VIE or acquires a portion of the primary beneficiary's interest in that entity.

An entity is deemed to be a VIE and thus to be consolidated, if, by intention, any one of the following conditions is present:

- The total equity investment at risk is insufficient to permit the entity to finance its activities without additional subordinated financial support from other parties (including equity holders).

- As a group, holders of the equity investment at risk (i.e., investors) lack any of the following characteristics of a controlling financial interest:

  — The direct or indirect ability to make significant decisions about the entity's activities through voting or similar rights.

  — The obligation to absorb the entity's expected losses; such an obligation does not exist if the holders/investors are directly or indirectly protected from losses or are guaranteed a return on their investment.

— The right to receive expected residual returns of the entity; that right is not considered to be present if the residual returns are capped by the entity's governing documents or by other arrangement.

Equity investors as a group are deemed to lack a characteristic of a controlling financial interest if (1) the voting rights of some investors are disproportionate to their obligations to absorb expected losses and/or their rights to receive expected residual returns, and (2) substantially all of the entity's activities either involve or are conducted on behalf of an investor having disproportionately few voting rights.

To qualify, total equity investment at risk:

- Includes only those equity interests that participate significantly in the entity's profits and losses (even if they carry no voting rights).

- Does not include equity interests that the entity issued in exchange for subordinated interests in other VIEs.

- Does not include amounts provided to the equity investor by the entity itself (or by other parties involved with the entity), unless the provider is a parent company, subsidiary, or affiliate of the investor that is (or is required to be) directly or indirectly consolidated with the investor.

- Does not include amounts financed for the equity investor (e.g., through loans or loan guarantees) directly by the entity itself or by other parties involved with the entity, unless that party is a parent, subsidiary or affiliate of the investor that is (or is required to be) consolidated with the investor.

The initial determination of whether an entity is a VIE should be made as of the date on which an enterprise becomes involved with the entity through ownership or through contractual or other pecuniary (monetary) interests. Determination should be based on circumstances existing on that date and on future changes that are required by the entity's governing documents and by current contractual arrangements. The initial determination should be reconsidered only if one or more of the following takes place:

- The entity's governing documents or contractual arrangements among the parties involved are changed in a way that changes the characteristics or adequacy of the investment at risk.

- Some or all of the equity investment is returned to investors, and other parties become exposed to expected losses.

- The entity undertakes additional activities or acquires additional assets beyond those anticipated at the later of (1) inception of the entity, or (2) the latest reconsideration date that increase expected losses.

- The entity receives an additional equity interest at risk or the entity curtails or modifies its activities in a way that decreases its expected losses.

In general, assets and liabilities and non-controlling interests should be measured (consolidated) at their fair values as of the date the enterprise first qualifies as the primary beneficiary. After initial measurement, normal consolidation principles apply (including the elimination of intercompany transactions and balances). In the consolidated statements, a VIE's net income or loss should be attributed to the primary beneficiary, rather than to the non-controlling interests.

# ¶ 2205. Special Purpose Entities

A transfer of all or a portion of financial assets should be accounted for as a sale, provided that the transferor surrenders control over the assets. When financial assets are transferred to a special purpose entity (SPE), such entity must be consolidated with the transferor unless the SPE is deemed a "qualifying" SPE (QSPE). A qualifying SPE is a trust or other legal vehicle that meets all of the following conditions:

- It is demonstrably different from the transferor such that it cannot be unilaterally dissolved by the transferor (or its affiliates or agents) and either (1) at least 10% of the fair value of the beneficial interests is held by parties other than the transferor (or its affiliates or agents), or (2) the transfer is a guaranteed mortgage securitization.
- Its permitted activities (1) are significantly limited, (2) are entirely specified in legal documents establishing it or creating the beneficial interests in the transferred assets it holds, and (3) may be substantially modified only upon approval of at least a majority of the beneficial interests held by parties other than the transferor (or its affiliates or agents).
- It may hold only the following:

  — Passive financial assets transferred to it (i.e., the assets do not involve the holder in decisions apart from those inherent in servicing the assets).

  — Passive derivative financial instruments pertaining to beneficial interests (including such an instrument that is itself a derivative instrument) issued or sold to parties other than the transferor (or its affiliates or agents).

  — Financial assets (e.g., guarantees or rights to collateral) that would reimburse it if others were to fail to service financial assets transferred to it or to pay obligations due it.

  — Servicing rights related to the financial assets it holds.

  — Non-financial assets obtained in connection with collection of the financial assets it holds (but only temporarily).

  — Cash collected from assets it holds and investments purchased with that cash pending distribution to beneficial interests; such investments must be appropriate for the purpose of distribution (e.g., money-market or other relatively risk-free instruments without options and with maturity dates no later than the expected date of distribution).

- If the SPE may sell or otherwise dispose of non-cash financial assets transferred to it, it may do so only in automatic response to one of the following situations:

  — The occurrence of an event or circumstance that (1) is specified in legal documents establishing the SPE or creating the beneficial interests in the transferred assets it holds, (2) is outside the control of the transferor (or its affiliates or agents), and (3) causes (or at the date of transfer is expected to cause) the fair value of the non-cash financial assets to decline by a specified degree below the fair value of such assets at the time they were obtained (e.g., the obligor's default, a downgrade by a major rating agency, the transferor's involuntary insolvency, inadequate servicing of the financial assets that could result in the loss of a third-party credit guarantee).

— The use of discretion in disposing of foreclosed assets if the discretion is significantly limited and spelled out in the legal documents establishing the SPE.

— The use of discretion regarding the disposal of loans, provided that the servicing agreement in effect when the SPE was established describes the specific conditions under which the servicer is required to dispose of such loans.

— Exercise by a beneficial interest holder (other than the transferor, its affiliates, or agents) of a right to put the holder's beneficial interest back to the SPE in exchange for (1) a full or partial distribution of the assets, (2) cash, which may require the SPE to dispose of the transferred assets or to issue new beneficial interests to fund settlement of the put, or (3) new beneficial interests.

— Exercise by the transferor of a call or a removal-of-accounts provision (ROAP) specified in legal documents that established the SPE or that created the beneficial interests.

— Termination of the SPE or the maturity of the beneficial interests in the non-cash financial assets on a fixed or determinable basis specified at inception.

IFRS

## ¶ 2206. Main Authoritative Sources

- IAS 27, *Consolidated and Separate Financial Statements*
- SIC 12, *Consolidation—Special Purpose Entities*

## ¶ 2207. Consolidated Statements in General

Consolidated financial statements should include all of the parent company's subsidiaries. A subsidiary is defined as an entity, including an unincorporated entity that is controlled by another entity (referred to as the parent).

Control of one entity by another is presumed to exist when the parent owns (directly or indirectly) more than 50% of the voting power of the entity unless, in exceptional circumstances, it can be clearly demonstrated that such ownership does not constitute control. Control is also deemed to exist when the parent owns 50% or less of the voting power of an entity but has the power:

- Over more than 50% of the voting rights by virtue of an agreement with other investors.
- To govern the financial and operating policies of the entity under a statute or equivalent governing body and control of the entity is by that board or body.

- To cast the majority of votes at meetings of the board of directors or equivalent governing body and control of the entity is by that board or body.

- To appoint or remove the majority of the members of the board of directors or equivalent governing body and control of the entity is by that board or body

The financial statements of the parent and its subsidiaries should be as of the same reporting date. When the reporting dates of the parent and a subsidiary are different, financial statements for the subsidiary should be prepared to coincide with the date of the parent's statements. If it is impracticable to do so, the difference between the reporting date of the subsidiary's financial statement and those of the parent's should be no more than three months. Intra-group balances and transactions should be eliminated in full.

Minority interests represent the portion of the profit or loss and net assets of a subsidiary attributable to equity interests that are not owned by the parent. Minority interests should be presented in the consolidated balance sheet within stockholders' equity, separately from the parent shareholders' equity. Minority interests in the profit or loss of the group should also be separately disclosed.

Note: In January 2008, the IASB issued revised IAS 27, which becomes effective from July 1, 2009, with early adoption allowed. Following are the principal changes from the previous standard:

- Changes in a parent's ownership interest in a subsidiary that do not result in the loss of control are accounted for as equity transactions (i.e., no gain or loss is recognized).

- When a parent loses control of a subsidiary, assets, liabilities, and the non-controlling interest in the subsidiary are derecognized, with any retained interest in the former subsidiary recognized and measured at fair value.

Consolidated total comprehensive income must be attributable to the noncontrolling interest (even if doing so results in a negative balance).

# ¶ 2208. Combined Statements

IFRS does not address the topic of combined financial statements.

# ¶ 2209. Variable Interest Entities

IFRS does not address the topic of variable interest entities.

# ¶ 2210. Special Purpose Entities

A special purpose entity (SPE) should be consolidated when the substance of the relationship between another entity and the SPE indicates that the SPE is controlled by that entity. Control may exist even when an entity owns little or none of the SPE's equity. The following in-substance circumstances may indicate a relationship in which an entity controls an SPE and consequently should consolidate the SPE:

- The activities of the SPE are being conducted on behalf of the entity according to its specific business needs so that the entity obtains benefits from the SPE's operation.
- The entity has the decision-making powers to obtain the majority of the benefits of the activities of the SPE or the entity has delegated these decision-making powers.
- The entity has rights to obtain the majority of the benefits of the SPE and therefore may be exposed to risks incident to the activities of the SPE.
- The entity retains the majority of the residual or ownership risks related to the SPE or its assets in order to obtain benefits from its activities.

# ¶ 2300. Contingencies and Provisions

## U.S. GAAP

## ¶ 2301. Main Authoritative Sources

- SFAS No. 5, *Accounting for Contingencies*
- SFAS No. 143, *Accounting for Asset Retirement Obligations*
- SFAS No. 146, *Accounting for Costs Associated with Exit or Disposal Activities*
- FASB Interpretation No. 24, *Reasonable Estimation of the Amount of a Loss*
- FASB Interpretation No. 45, *Guarantor's Accounting and Disclosure Requirements for Guarantees, Including Indirect Guarantees of Indebtedness of Others*
- FASB Interpretation No. 47, *Accounting for Conditional Asset Retirement Obligations*
- SOP No. 96-1, *Environmental Remediation Liabilities*

## ¶ 2302. Contingent Liabilities and Assets

A contingency is defined as an existing condition, situation, or set of circumstances involving uncertainty as to a possible gain or loss that will ultimately be resolved when one or more future events occur or fail to occur. An estimated loss from a contingency should be accrued and charged to operations only if both of the following conditions are met:

- Information available prior to the issuance of the financial statements indicates that it is probable (virtual certainty is not required) that an asset has been impaired or a liability incurred as of the date of the financial statements.
- The amount of the loss can be reasonably estimated.

Reasonable estimation of the possible loss does not mean that it is necessary to estimate one single amount; rather, a loss should be accrued if it can be estimated within a range. If some amount within the range appears to be a better estimate than any other amount within the range, that amount should be accrued. If no amount within the range is a better estimate than any other amount, the minimum amount in the range should be accrued.

When a loss contingency exists, the likelihood that the occurrence (or failure thereof) of a future event will confirm the loss ranges from remote to probable, as follows:

- Remote. The chance of the future event occurring is slight.
- Reasonably possible. The chance of the future event occurring is more than remote but less than likely.
- Probable. The future event is likely to occur.

Accrual of an expected loss should be made only when it is probable that the future event will occur to confirm the loss (and it meets the other conditions of reasonable estimation of the amount as discussed above). If one or both conditions are not met, but there is at least a reasonable possibility that a loss has been incurred, disclosure is required. If the possibility that a loss has been incurred is remote, disclosure may also be required. An estimated gain from a contingency should *not* be recorded until the gain is realized.

## ¶ 2303. Guarantees

At inception of a guarantee having one or more of the following characteristics, the guarantor must recognize a liability for the obligation:

- Contracts contingently requiring payment (in cash, other assets, shares of stock, or financial instruments) to the guaranteed party, based on changes in the price of an under-lying that is related to an asset or liability of the guaranteed party.

- Contracts contingently requiring payment to the guaranteed party, based on another entity's failure to perform pursuant to an obligating agreement (a performance guarantee).

- Indemnification agreements contingently requiring payment to the indemnified party, based on changes in an under-lying related to an asset, a liability, or an equity security of the guaranteed party (e.g., an adverse outcome of a lawsuit, an adverse ruling in a tax matter, the imposition of additional taxes caused by changes in tax laws).

- Indirect guarantees of the indebtedness of others.

The liability for the obligation should be measured at inception as follows:

- If the guarantee is issued in a standalone arm's-length transaction, the amount of the liability recognized should, as a practical expedient, be equal to the premium received or due from the guaranteed party.

- If the guarantee is issued as part of a multiple-element transaction (e.g., in conjunction with the sale of equipment by the guarantor to a customer, accompanied by a guarantee of the customer's bank loan for which the proceeds are used to pay for the equipment), the amount of the liability recognized at inception should be its fair value, which may be as a practical expedient equal to the premium that would be required by the guarantor in a standalone arm's-length transaction.

- For a guarantee that may have uncertainties both as to timing and amount, the liability should be initially recorded at fair value using the expected value technique for estimating the amount.

The initial amount recognized should be reduced (with a corresponding credit to earnings) as the guarantor is released from risk (1) upon expiration or settlement of the obligation, (2) through systematic amortization over the term of the obligation, or (3) as the fair value of the guarantee changes from period to period.

## ¶ 2304. Provisions

There is no authoritative U.S. GAAP pronouncement that covers the general topic of provisions; rather, explicit rules exist for the recognition, measurement, and disclosure of specific liabilities. A provision is defined in IAS No. 37, *Provisions, Contingent Liabilities and Contingent Assets*, as a liability of uncertain timing or amount that should be recognized when (1) the entity has a present obligation arising from past events, (2) it is probable that an outflow of resources embodying economic benefits will be required to settle the obligation, and (3) a reliable estimate of the obligation can be made.

## ¶ 2305. Asset Retirement Obligations

An asset retirement obligation (ARO) is defined as an obligation associated with the sale, abandonment, disposal, or other non-temporary removal from operation of a long-term tangible asset arising from the acquisition, construction, or development and/or the normal operation of a long-lived asset. An ARO should be recognized at fair value when it is incurred—but only if a reasonable estimate of its fair value can be made at that time; otherwise, the obligation should be recorded when fair value can be reasonably estimated. An incremental liability (i.e., one that is incurred over more than one accounting period because events creating it occur over time) should be recognized at fair value as an additional layer of the original liability.

An ARO includes a legal obligation to perform an asset retirement activity in which the timing and/or method of settlement are conditional on a future event that may not be within the control of the entity (i.e., under those circumstances, the obligation itself is unconditional, even though uncertainty about timing or manner of settlement exists). Thus, a liability for the fair value of a conditional ARO should be recognized when incurred if the fair value of the liability can be reasonably estimated.

Fair value of ARO is subject to reasonable estimation if (1) it is evident that the fair value is embodied in the acquisition price of the related asset; (2) an active market exists for the transfer of the obligation; or (3) there is sufficient information available to apply an expected present value technique that incorporates uncertainty about timing and method of settlement into the measurement of fair value. When an ARO is recognized, the amount of the liability should be correspondingly added to the carrying amount of the related long-lived asset. The amount to be charged to operations each period (i.e., depreciation) should be based on a systematic and rational allocation method.

When testing the related asset for impairment, the carrying amount should include capitalized asset retirement costs, but future cash flows related to the ARO should be excluded from estimates of both undiscounted cash inflows (for purposes of performing the recoverability test) and from discounted cash inflows to determine the asset's fair value (for purposes of measuring the impairment loss). If fair value of the asset being tested for impairment is based on a quoted market price (which presumably incorporates the projected costs of retiring the asset), the market price should be increased by the fair value of the ARO when measuring impairment.

Although initially measured at fair value, subsequent measurement of an ARO should be based on a method of allocation such that period-to-period increases or decreases in the liability are recognized due to (1) the passage of time, and (2) revisions to the timing and/or amount of the original estimate of undiscounted cash outflows.

Changes in the ARO resulting from revisions to the timing or the amount of the original estimate of undiscounted cash outflows should also be recognized as an adjustment (an increase or decrease) to the carrying amount of the related asset.

## ¶ 2306. Environmental Costs

An environmental remediation liability should be recorded when it is probable that an asset has been impaired or a liability has been incurred. In this context, probability comprises the following elements:

- Litigation has commenced or a claim or an assessment has been asserted, or, based on available information, commencement of litigation or assertion of a claim or an assessment is probable.

- Based on available information, it is likely that the outcome of such litigation, claim, or assessment will be unfavorable.

For a liability to be accrued, the amount of the loss (including a range of loss) must be subject to reasonable estimates. When the overall liability is based on a range of estimated loss, the recorded amount may represent the lower end of a range of costs for some components of the liability and the best estimates within ranges of costs for other components. At the early stages of the remediation process, some components of the overall liability may not be reasonably estimable (which should not preclude recognition of a liability). In such a case, the components that are subject to reasonable estimation should be viewed as the minimum in the range of the overall liability. Likewise, uncertainties relating to the entity's *share* of an environmental remediation liability should not preclude the entity from recognizing its best estimate of its share of the liability or, if no best estimate can be made, the minimum estimate of its share of the liability, if the liability is probable and the total remediation liability associated with the site is reasonably estimable within a range.

The estimates of the liability should include the entity's:

- Allocable share of the liability for a specific site.

- Share of amounts that will not be paid by other potentially responsible parties or the government.

Costs to be included in the measurement of the environmental remediation liability are:

- Incremental direct costs of the remediation effort.

- Costs of compensation benefits for those employees who are expected to devote a significant amount of time directly to the remediation effort.

**WG&L**

For purposes of measuring the liability, estimates should be based on enacted laws and regulations; no changes should be anticipated. When such changes do occur, the impact thereof should be recognized at that time. The liability, or a component of the liability, may be discounted to reflect the time value of money if the aggregate amount of the liability (or a component) and the amount and timing of cash payments for the liability or component are fixed or reliably determinable. The amount of an environmental remediation liability should be determined independently from any potential claim for recovery, and an asset relating to the recovery should be recognized only when realization of the claim for recovery is deemed probable. If the claim is the subject of litigation, a rebuttable presumption exists that realization of the claim is not probable. The amount of potential recovery should be measured at fair value, which encompasses transaction costs related to receipt of the recovery and the time value of money. Discounting should not be applied to the amount of the recovery, however, if the liability is not discounted.

## ¶ 2307. Restructuring Costs

Under U.S. GAAP, the term "restructuring" or "restructuring costs" no longer appears in the formal literature; although such terms have been replaced in SFAS No. 146 by the term "exit activity," the guidance in SFAS No. 146 covers the accounting treatment for the following types of costs typically associated with restructurings:

- One-time termination benefits provided to current employees who are involuntarily terminated. Note that the benefits under an ongoing arrangement (including an enhancement to such an arrangement) do not qualify. Likewise the costs of benefits that are in-substance individual deferred compensation contracts do not qualify.

- Costs to terminate a contract (other than a capital lease).

- Other costs (including costs to consolidate facilities or to relocate employees).

Generally, a liability for a cost of an exit activity should be recognized when it becomes a present obligation (i.e., when a transaction or event occurs that leaves the entity little or no discretion to avoid future payment). The mere existence of an exit or disposal plan, of itself, does not create a present obligation. Initially, the liability should be measured at fair value. If fair value cannot be reasonably estimated when the liability is incurred, it should be recognized in the period in which fair value can be determined. In periods subsequent to initial recognition, changes to the liability are recorded to reflect the passage of time and to reflect any revisions to either the timing or the amount of estimated cash flows.

A one-time benefit arrangement is one established through a plan of termination that applies to a specified termination event or to a specified future period. A one-time benefit arrangement is deemed to be created as of the date the termination plan meets all of the following criteria *and* the details of which have been communicated to employees (referred to as the communication date):

- Management having the authority to approve the action commits to a plan of termination.
- The plan identifies (1) the number of employees to be terminated, (2) their job classifications or functions and locations, and (3) the anticipated completion date of the plan.
- The plan establishes the terms of the benefit arrangement (including cash and other benefits) in sufficient detail to enable employees to determine the type and amount of benefits they will receive if they are involuntarily terminated.
- Actions required to complete the plan indicate that it is unlikely that significant changes thereto will be made or that it will be withdrawn.

If employees are not required to render service until terminated in order to receive benefits or if they will not be retained beyond the minimum retention period (e.g., the minimum notification period required by law), a liability for one-time termination benefit costs should be recognized at fair value as of the communication date. If employees are required to render service until they are terminated and will in fact be retained to do so beyond the minimum retention period, the liability for one-time termination benefits should be initially measured as of the communication date based on fair value as of the termination date and recognized ratably over the future service period.

Contract termination costs comprise costs to terminate a contract before its term ends and/or continuing costs under the remaining term of a contract for which the entity receives no corresponding economic benefit. A liability for costs to terminate a contract prior to the end of its term should be measured at fair value and recognized when the contract is terminated.

Other costs associated with an exit or disposal activity (including costs to consolidate or close facilities and to relocate employees) should be recognized at fair value as of the date it is incurred (typically, when goods or services associated with the activity are received).

IFRS

## ¶ 2308. Main Authoritative Sources

- IAS 37, *Provisions, Contingent Liabilities and Contingent Assets*
- IAS 39, *Financial Instruments: Recognition and Measurement*
- IFRIC 1, *Changes in Existing Decommissioning, Restoration and Similar Liabilities*
- IFRIC 5, *Rights to Interests Arising from Decommissioning, Restoration and Environmental Rehabilitation Funds*
- IFRIC 6, *Liabilities Arising from Participating in a Specific Market—Waste Electrical and Electronic Equipment*

## ¶ 2309. Contingent Liabilities and Assets

A contingent liability is either:

- A possible obligation that arises from past events and whose existence will be confirmed only by the occurrence or non-occurrence of one or more uncertain future events not wholly within the control of the entity.
- A present obligation that arises from past events but is not recognized because (1) it is not probable that an outflow of resources embodying economic benefits will be required to settle the obligation, or (2) the amount of the obligation cannot be measured with sufficient reliability.

Contingent liabilities should not be recognized; rather, they should be disclosed unless the possibility of an outflow of resources embodying economic benefits is remote. Contingent liabilities should be assessed continually to determine whether an outflow of resources embodying economic benefits has become probable; if so, a provision should be recognized in the financial statements for the period in which the change in probability occurs.

A contingent asset is a possible asset that arises from past events and whose existence will be confirmed only by the occurrence or non-occurrence of one or more uncertain future events not wholly within the control of the entity. Contingent assets should not be recognized, but should be disclosed if an inflow of resources is deemed probable.

## ¶ 2310. Guarantees

A financial guarantee contract is a contract that requires the issuer to make specified payments to reimburse the holder for a loss it incurs because a specified debtor fails to make payment when due in accordance with the original or modified terms of a debt instrument. A financial guarantee contract should initially be measured at fair value, which, for a stand-alone guarantee, will normally be the amount of consideration received. Subsequently, it should be measured at the higher of (1) the amount expected to be paid, and (2) the amount initially recognized. A financial guarantee contract should be derecognized only when the liability is extinguished (i.e., when the obligation is discharged or cancelled or expires).

## ¶ 2311. Provisions

A provision is a liability of uncertain timing or amount. A provision should be recognized when:

- An entity has a present obligation (legal or constructive) as a result of a past event.
- It is probable that an outflow of resources embodying economic benefits will be required to settle the obligation. A reliable estimate can be made of the amount of the obligation.

A legal obligation is one that derives from:
- A contract (through its explicit or implicit terms).
- Legislation.
- Other operation of law.

A constructive obligation is one that derives from an entity's actions that:

- Through an established pattern of past practice, published policies, or a sufficiently specific current statement, the entity has indicated to other parties that it will accept certain responsibilities.

- As a result, the entity has created a valid expectation on the part of those other parties that it will discharge its responsibilities.

The amount recognized as a provision should be the best estimate of the expenditure required to settle the present obligation at the balance sheet date. If the effect of the time value of money is material, the amount of a provision should be discounted to its present value.

## ¶ 2312. Asset Retirement Obligations

Under IFRS, asset retirement obligations are referred to as decommissioning costs, which are obligations to dismantle, remove, and restore items of property, plant and equipment. A provision (i.e., a liability) for decommissioning costs should be recognized, and initially measured at its present value, when the obligation to dismantle, remove, and restore is established. A corresponding amount should be charged to the related asset.

Accounting for subsequent changes attributable to changes in the estimated timing or amount of the obligation depends on whether the cost model or the revaluation model is applied to the related asset. If the cost model is used, such changes should be added to or deducted from the carrying value of the liability (and, correspondingly, to the carrying value of the related asset). Under the revaluation model, subsequent decreases in the liability should be credited directly to revaluation surplus; subsequent increases in the liability should be taken directly to profit and loss.

In some situations, an entity's obligation for decommissioning costs may be settled (either voluntarily or by law) through contributions to a fund administered by an independent trustee. A liability for required contributions to the fund should be recognized, together with the entity's interest in the fund (unless the entity has no obligation to pay decommissioning costs in the event the fund fails to pay them). If the entity has control or joint control of, or significant influence over the fund, its interest should be accounted for accordingly; otherwise, the entity's right to receive reimbursement from the fund should be measured at the lower of (1) the amount of the decommissioning liability recognized, or (2) the entity's share of the fair value of the net assets of the fund attributable to all contributors. Changes in the carrying amount of the right to receive reimbursements (other than contributions to and payments from the fund) should be recognized in profit and loss.

When a contributor has an obligation to make potential additional contributions (e.g., in the event of the bankruptcy of another contributor or if the value of the investment assets held by the fund decreases to an extent that they are insufficient to fulfill the fund's reimbursement obligations), such obligation is a contingent liability to be recognized only if it is probable that additional contributions will be made.

## ¶ 2313. Environmental Costs

A liability for clean-up costs or penalties from unlawful environmental damage should be established under the following circumstances:

- The obligation arose from past events existing independently of the entity's future actions.
- A new law is passed requiring existing damage to be rectified.
- The entity publicly accepts responsibility for rectification in a way that creates a constructive obligation.

In respect of waste management for equipment sold to private households before August 13, 2005 (pursuant to a European Union Directive that regulates the collection, treatment, recovery, and environmentally sound disposal of waste equipment), the obligating event (and thus when a liability should be recognized) occurs when the selling entity has participated in the market (i.e., has established a market share), rather than when the products may have been manufactured or sold. Hence, the timing of the obligating event may be different from the period in which the activities to perform the waste management are undertaken and the related costs incurred.

## ¶ 2314. Restructuring Costs

A restructuring is defined as a program that is planned and controlled by management and materially changes either:

- The scope of a business undertaken by an entity.
- The manner in which the business is conducted.

The following are examples of events that may fall under the definition of restructuring program:

- The sale or termination of a line of business.
- The closure of business locations in a country or region or the relocation of business activities from one country or region to another.
- Changes in management structure.
- Fundamental reorganizations that have a material effect on the nature and focus of the entity's operations.

A provision for restructuring costs should be recognized when the following general recognition criteria for provisions are met:

- A present obligation (legal or constructive) exists as a result of a past event.
- It is probable that an outflow of resources embodying economic benefits will be required to settle the obligation.
- A reliable estimate can be made of the amount of the obligation.

A constructive obligation to restructure arises only when an entity:

- Has a detailed formal plan for the restructuring that identifies (1) the business or part of a business concerned, (2) the principal locations affected, (3) the location, function, and approximate number of employees who will be compensated for terminating their services, (4) the expenditures that will be undertaken, and (5) when the plan will be implemented.

- Has raised a valid expectation in those affected that it will carry out the restructuring by starting to implement that plan or announcing its main features to those affected by it.

Note that a constructive obligation in respect of the sale of an operation does not arise until the entity is committed to the sale (i.e., there is a binding sale agreement).

A restructuring provision should include only the direct expenditures arising from the restructuring that are both:

- Necessarily entailed by the restructuring.
- Not associated with the ongoing activities of the entity.

# ¶ 2400. Derivatives and Hedging

U.S. GAAP

## ¶ 2401. Main Authoritative Sources

- SFAS No. 133, *Accounting for Derivative Instruments and Hedging Activities*

## ¶ 2402. Derivatives

A derivative is a financial instrument that possesses all three of the following characteristics:

- It has one or more "underlying" and one or more "notional" (or face) amount or payment provision. An underlying is a specified rate, price, index of prices or rates, or other variable, including the occurrence or nonoccurrence of a specified event (e.g., the scheduled payment under a contract). A notional amount is a specified number of shares, bushels, pounds, currency units, or other measure.

- It requires either no initial net investment or an initial net investment that is smaller than would otherwise be required for other types of contracts expected to have a similar response to changes in market factors.

- Its terms require or permit net settlement (but there is a market mechanism that facilitates settlement), it can readily be settled by a means outside the contract (i.e., neither party is required to deliver an asset associated with the character of the underlying or notional amount), or it provides for delivery of an asset that places the recipient in a position not substantially different from net settlement (i.e., the asset is readily convertible into cash).

Contracts that do not themselves meet the criteria of a derivative, such as bonds, notes, insurance policies, or leases, may nevertheless contain so-called embedded derivatives. An embedded derivative either implicitly or explicitly modifies some or all of the cash flows or the value of exchanges otherwise required of the counterparties. Embedded derivatives must be separated from their host contracts and accounted for as derivatives if all of the following criteria are met:

- The economic characteristics and risks of the embedded derivatives are not clearly and closely related to those of the host contract;

- The contract that embodies both the embedded derivative and the host (the hybrid instrument) is not, pursuant to otherwise applicable GAAP, remeasured at fair value with changes in fair value reported in current earnings; and

- A separate instrument with the same terms as the embedded instrument would qualify as a self-standing derivative.

Derivatives that are not considered hedges must be recognized in the balance sheet at fair value, with changes in fair value reflected in current earnings.

## ¶ 2403. Fair Value Hedges

For a qualifying fair value hedge:

- Any gain or loss on the hedging instrument is recognized in current earnings.

- Any gain or loss on the hedged item attributable to the hedged risk is recognized in current earnings, with a corresponding change in the carrying amount of the hedged item.

If the hedge is fully effective, the gain or loss on the hedging instrument would exactly offset the loss or gain on the hedged item. Note, though, that as permitted, a specific element of gain or loss on the hedging instrument (derivative) may be excluded from the assessment of the hedge's effectiveness. The excluded portion of the hedging instrument's gain or loss, along with any gain or loss arising from hedge ineffectiveness (based on management's defined risk strategy), should be reported as a credit (gain) or charge (loss) to earnings in the current period.

If the hedged item is required to be measured at fair value pursuant to GAAP (e.g., an available-for-sale security), the adjustment of the hedged item's carrying amount should nevertheless be recognized in current earnings (rather than in comprehensive income). Recognition in current earnings is necessary to offset the gain or loss on the hedging instrument.

Accounting for a qualifying item as a fair value hedge should be discontinued when any of the following conditions are present:

- Designation as a hedge is removed.

- The hedging instrument is sold, terminated, or exercised.

- The criteria for qualification of the hedging instrument, the hedging relationship, or the hedged item are no longer met.

## ¶ 2404. Cash Flow Hedges

For a qualifying cash flow hedge:

- The component of the gain or loss on the hedging instrument that has been excluded from the assessment of hedge effectiveness, if any, is recognized in current earnings.

- The effective portion of the gain or loss on the hedging instrument is reported in other comprehensive income.

Reclassification into earnings from accumulated other comprehensive income should be made in the same period(s) during which the hedged forecasted transaction affects earnings (e.g., when depreciation expense, interest expense, or cost of sales is recognized). If, however, it appears that continued reporting of a loss in accumulated other comprehensive income will lead to recognizing a net loss in future periods (i.e., a loss on the combination of the hedging instrument and the hedged transaction), a loss representing the expected unrecovered amount should be reclassified into current earnings.

Cash flow hedge accounting should be discontinued under any of the following circumstances:

- Designation as a hedge is removed.
- The hedging instrument is sold, terminated or exercised.
- The criteria for qualification of the hedging instrument, the hedging relationship, or the hedged item are no longer met.

## ¶ 2405. Foreign Currency Hedges

In general, the following types of hedges of foreign currency exposure may be designated:

- A fair value hedge of an unrecognized firm commitment or a recognized asset or liability (including an available-for-sale security); such a hedge is accounted for in the same manner as other fair value hedges.
- A cash flow hedge of a forecasted transaction, an unrecognized firm commitment, the forecasted functional currency equivalent cash flows associated with a recognized asset or liability, or an intercompany transaction; such a hedge is accounted for in the same manner as other cash flow hedges.
- A hedge of a net investment in a foreign operation; the gain or loss on such a hedge (which may be either a derivative or non-derivative financial instrument) should be reported in the same manner as the translation adjustment.

IFRS

## ¶ 2406. Main Authoritative Sources

- IAS 29, *Financial Instruments: Recognition and Measurement*

## ¶ 2407. Derivatives

A derivative is a financial instrument or other contract having all three of the following characteristics:

- Its value changes in response to the change in a specified interest rate, financial instrument price, commodity price, foreign exchange rate, index of prices or rates, credit rating or credit index, or other variable (sometimes referred to as the "underlying").
- It requires no initial net investment or an initial net investment that is smaller than would be required for other types of contracts that would be expected to have a similar response to changes in market factors.
- It is settled at a future date.

An embedded derivative is a component of a hybrid (combined) instrument that also includes a non-derivative host contract (with the effect that some of the cash flows of the combined instrument vary in a way similar to a stand-alone derivative). An embedded derivative causes some or all of the cash flows that otherwise would be required by the contract to be modified according to an underlying.

An embedded derivative must be separated from the host contract and accounted for as a derivative if:

- The economic characteristics and risks of the embedded derivative are not closely related to the economic characteristics and risks of the host contract.

- A separate instrument with the same terms as the embedded derivative would meet the definition of a derivative.

- The hybrid (combined) instrument is not measured at fair value with changes in fair value recognized in profit or loss.

Derivatives that do not qualify for hedge accounting should be recognized on the balance sheet at fair value; subsequent changes in fair value should be recognized in profit or loss.

## ¶ 2408. Fair Value Hedges

A qualifying fair value hedge should be accounted for as follows:

- The gain or loss from remeasuring the hedging instrument at fair value should be recognized in profit or loss.

- The gain or loss on the hedged item attributable to the hedged risk should adjust the carrying amount of the hedged item and be recognized in profit or loss; note that this applies even if the hedged item is an available-for-sale instrument whose gain or loss is otherwise recognized in equity (i.e., to offset the gain or loss on the hedging instrument).

Fair value hedge accounting should be discontinued when:

- The hedging instrument expires or is sold, terminated, or exercised.
- The hedge no longer meets the criteria for hedge accounting.
- The entity revokes the hedge designation.

## ¶ 2409. Cash Flow Hedges

A qualifying cash flow hedge should be accounted for in the following manner:

- The portion of the gain or loss on the hedging instrument that is determined to be an effective hedge should be recognized directly in equity.

- The ineffective portion of the gain or loss on the hedging instrument should be recognized in profit or loss.

If a hedge of a forecast transaction subsequently results in recognition of a financial asset or a financial liability, the associated gains or losses that were recognized directly in equity should be reclassified into profit or loss in the same period(s) during which the asset acquired or liability assumed affects profit or loss (e.g., when interest income or interest expense is recognized). If, however, an entity expects that all or a portion of a loss recognized directly in equity will not be recovered in one or more future periods, the amount not expected to be recovered should be reclassified into profit or loss.

Cash flow hedge accounting should be discontinued under the following circumstances:

- The hedging instrument expires or is sold, terminated, or exercised.
- The hedge no longer meets the criteria for hedge accounting.
- The forecast transaction is no longer expected to occur.
- Designation of a hedge is removed.

## ¶ 2410. Foreign Currency Hedges

In general, foreign currency hedges should be accounted for, as applicable, in the same manner as other fair value or cash flow hedges; hedges of a net investment in a foreign operation, including a hedge of a monetary item accounted for as part of the net investment, should be accounted for similarly to cash flow hedges (i.e., the portion of the gain or loss on the hedging instrument determined to be an effective hedge is recognized directly in equity, and the ineffective portion is recognized in profit or loss).

# ¶ 2500. Development Stage Entities

## U.S. GAAP

## ¶ 2501. Main Authoritative Sources

- SFAS No. 7, *Accounting and Reporting by Development Stage Enterprises*

A company is considered to be in the development stage if it is devoting substantially all of its efforts to establishing a new business and either its (1) planned principal operations have not started, or (2) planned principal operations are underway but have not yet generated any significant revenue.

GAAP applies to development stage companies as well as to operating companies. Revenue recognition and capitalization or expensing of costs for companies in the development stage should be determined based on the substance of the transactions just as they would for mature enterprises. It is possible that an item that would be capitalized (as an asset) on the balance sheet of a mature company would be expensed in the income statement of a development stage company, because the recoverability of costs must be assessed within the environment of a specific entity.

In addition to other applicable required disclosures, development stage entities must:

- Identify the financial statements as those of a development stage company.
- Provide a description of the development stage activities in which the company is engaged.
- Present a statement of stockholders' equity from inception that includes for each issuance (1) the dollar amounts assigned to the consideration received for equity securities, and (2) the date and number of shares of equity securities issued for cash and for non-cash consideration (and for each issuance involving non-cash consideration, the nature of that consideration and the basis for assigning amounts).
- Disclose in the equity section of the balance sheet, the amount of deficit accumulated in the development stage.
- Disclose on the face of the income statement, the amounts of revenue and expenses for each period covered, as well as cumulative amounts of revenue and expenses since inception.
- Present a cash flow statement showing cash inflows and cash outflows for each period covered and cumulative amounts of each since inception.

In the first year in which the company is considered an operating company, a statement should be made that, in prior years, it had been in the development stage. When comparative statements include periods in which the company was first in the development stage and later an operating company, the cumulative amounts and other disclosures are not required for the periods in which the company was in the development stage.

IFRS

## ¶ 2502. Main Authoritative Sources

- None - not directly addressed

# ¶ 2600. Foreign Operations

## U.S. GAAP

## ¶ 2601. Main Authoritative Sources

- SFAS No. 52, *Foreign Currency Translation*
- FASB Interpretation No. 37, *Accounting for Translation Adjustments upon Sale of Part of an Investment in a Foreign Entity*

## ¶ 2602. Translation of Foreign Currency Financial Statements

Financial statements of a subsidiary that are stated on the subsidiary's functional currency should be translated using the current rate method. A foreign company's functional currency is the currency of the primary economic environment in which it operates. Normally, that will be the currency of the country in which the company generates and expends cash. The current rate method requires that all accounts in foreign financial statements be translated using the current exchange rate, which is applied differently for various elements of financial statements, as follows:

- *Assets and liabilities* are translated at the rate in effect on the date of the financial statements (i.e., the spot rate).
- *Revenues and expenses* are translated at the weighted average rate for the period.
- *Gains and losses* are translated at the weighted average rate for the period.
- *Accounting allocations* (e.g., depreciation, amortization) are translated at the rate in effect when the allocation was made (i.e., not at the rate in effect when the related item originated).
- *Capital stock and additional paid-in capital* are translated at the rate in effect when the shares were issued.
- *Retained earnings* is a calculated amount, which equals the beginning balance (i.e., the prior period's calculated amount), plus the amount of translated net income for the current period, minus the amount of dividends (which are translated at the rate in effect on the dates of declaration).

The use of various exchange rates in the translation process gives rise to a translation adjustment, which should be reported in accumulated comprehensive income. When part or all of a company's ownership interest in a foreign entity is sold, a pro rata portion of the accumulated translation adjustment attributable to that entity should be recognized in determining any gain or loss on the sale.

When a foreign company's financial statements are not stated in the entity's functional currency, remeasurement is required before translation. The remeasurement process requires use of historical exchange rates to translate nonmonetary assets and liabilities (and related revenue and expense accounts), with current rates used for all other items. Unlike the translation adjustment, which is reported as a component of equity through accumulated comprehensive income, the remeasurement adjustment should be reported as a component of income or loss for the period.

Financial statements of a foreign company that operates in a highly inflationary economy should be remeasured into U.S. dollars. A highly inflationary economy is defined as one that has cumulative inflation of approximately 100% or more over a three-year period.

## ¶ 2603. Foreign Currency Transactions

Gains or losses resulting from the effect of exchange rate changes on transactions denominated in currencies other than the functional currency are generally included in determining net income for the period in which exchange rates change, unless the transaction hedges a foreign currency commitment or a net investment in a foreign entity. The amount of gain or loss on a hedge against a firm foreign currency commitment should be deferred and included in the measurement of the related foreign currency transaction. Foreign currency transactions that are designated as, and are effective as, economic hedges of a net investment in a foreign entity are treated in the same manner as a translation adjustment (i.e., as a component of accumulated comprehensive income), as are intercompany foreign currency transactions that are of a long-term-investment nature (i.e., settlement is not planned or anticipated in the foreseeable future).

IFRS

## ¶ 2604. Main Authoritative Sources

- IAS 23, *The Effects of Changes in Foreign Exchange Rates*
- IAS 29, *Financial Reporting in Hyperinflationary Economies*

## ¶ 2605. Translation of Foreign Currency Financial Statements

An entity may present its financial statements in any currency. If the presentation currency differs from the entity's functional currency (i.e., the currency of the primary economic environment in which the entity operates), its financial statements should be translated into the presentation currency, as follows:

- *Assets and liabilities* are translated at the closing rate at the date of that balance sheet (the closing rate).
- *Income and expenses* are translated at exchange rates at the dates of the transactions (or, for practical reasons, the average rate for the period).
- *Resulting exchange differences* from using different translation rates are included as a separate component of equity.

The financial statements of a foreign entity whose books and records are kept in other than its functional currency should be translated using the current rate for monetary items and historical rates for nonmonetary items, with any resulting translation gain or loss recognized in profit and loss. When a foreign entity's functional currency is that of a hyperinflationary economy (one in which the cumulative inflation rate over three years is approaching or exceeds 100%), the entity's financial statements must first be restated in terms of the measuring unit current at the balance sheet date before they are translated into the presentation currency. Restatement is accomplished as follows:

- Balance sheet items not already stated at current cost (i.e., monetary assets and liabilities) should be restated by applying a general price index.
- Income statement items are restated by applying the change in the general price index from the dates on which the items were initially recorded.
- Gain or loss on the net monetary position (which may be estimated by applying the price index change to the weighted average net monetary position for the period) should be included in profit and loss.

## ¶ 2606. Foreign Currency Transactions

Exchange differences arising from the settlement of monetary items (or upon translation of such items at subsequent reporting dates) at rates different from those at which they were initially recorded should be recognized in profit or loss in the period in which they occur, except that exchange differences arising on a monetary item that is a net investment in a foreign operation should be recognized as a separate component of stockholders' equity and included in profit and loss on disposal of the net investment.

# ¶ 2700. Government Grants

## U.S. GAAP

## ¶ 2701. Main Authoritative Sources

- None—not directly addressed

Although no authoritative pronouncements exist covering accounting for government grants and assistance, by analogy, they are accounted for as follows:

- If the grant is in the form of revenue, it should be recognized during the period that the related expenditure is made.
- If the grant is for research and development costs, it should be accounted for as a reduction of the related R&D expense.
- If the grant relates to a capital expenditure (i.e., for the acquisition or construction of an asset), it should be reflected as either (1) a deferred credit that is amortized over the period during which the asset is depreciated, or (2) a reduction of the asset's carrying value.

## IFRS

## ¶ 2702. Main Authoritative Sources

- IAS 20, *Accounting for Government Grants and Disclosure of Government Assistance*
- SIC 10, *Government Assistance—No Specific Relation to Operating Activities*

Government grants are defined as assistance by a government in the form of transfers of resources to an entity in return for past or future compliance with certain conditions relating to the operating activities of that entity. They exclude forms of government assistance that cannot reasonably have a value placed on them and transactions with governments that cannot be distinguished from the normal trading transactions of the entity.

A government grant, including a nonmonetary grant at fair value, should not be recognized until there is reasonable assurance that:

- The entity will comply with the conditions attaching to the grant.
- The grant will be received.

A government grant should be recognized as income, on a systematic basis, over the periods necessary to match it with the related costs it is intended to compensate (e.g., a grant related to depreciable assets is usually recognized as income over the periods to which depreciation on those assets is charged). A government grant may not be credited directly to stockholders' equity, even if there are no conditions specifically relating to the entity's operating activities (other than the requirement to do business in certain regions or industry sectors). A government grant that becomes receivable as compensation for expenses or losses already incurred or for the purpose of giving immediate financial support to the entity with no future related costs should be recognized in income during the period in which it becomes receivable. A government grant related to assets may be presented in the balance sheet either by establishing a deferred income account or by deducting the amount of the grant in arriving at the carrying amount of the asset.

A government grant that becomes repayable should be accounted for as a revision to an accounting estimate. Repayment of a grant related to income should be recognized immediately as an expense. Repayment of a grant related to an asset should be accounted for by increasing the carrying amount of the asset or by reducing the deferred income balance (as applicable). The cumulative additional depreciation that would have been recognized to date as an expense in the absence of the grant shall be recognized immediately as an expense.

# ¶ 2800. Interim Reporting

## U.S. GAAP

## ¶ 2801. Main Authoritative Sources

- APB Opinion No. 28, *Interim Financial Reporting*

Each interim period should be considered as an integral part of an annual period. Results of operations for each interim period should be based on the accounting principles and practices used in the preparation of the latest annual financial statements unless a change in an accounting policy or practice has been adopted in the current year. Certain accounting principles and practices followed for annual reporting purposes may, however, need to be modified for interim reporting so that interim results may better relate to results for the entire year.

In general, costs and expenses should be charged against income in interim periods as incurred, or, if appropriate, allocated among interim periods based on an estimate of time expired or benefit received. If a cost or expense is charged against income for annual purposes but benefits more than one interim period, it should be allocated among these interim periods. Those costs and expenses that are typically subjected to year-end adjustment (e.g., year-end bonuses, allowance for doubtful accounts, depreciation) should be adjusted (to the extent possible) for interim results.

Generally, cost of sales should be determined in the same manner as that used for the full year with the following exceptions: (1) the gross profit method may be used to determine interim inventory costs; (2) if a LIFO liquidation occurs at an interim date but is expected to be replaced by the end of the year, cost of sales should include the expected cost of replacement of the liquidated LIFO base; (3) inventory losses from market declines should be recognized in the interim period in which they occur, and recoveries of such losses in later interim periods of the same year should be recognized in those periods; (4) temporary market declines should be recognized unless substantial evidence exists that market prices will recover before the inventory is sold; and (5) inventory and product costs determined by a standard cost system in annual statements should be determined in the same manner for interim statements, except that planned variances that are expected to be absorbed by the end of the year should not be included.

A change in accounting principle made in an interim period should be reported in the period in which the change occurs. The effect of a change in accounting estimate should be accounted for in the period in which the change is made.

## IFRS

## ¶ 2802. Main Authoritative Sources

- IAS 34, *Interim Financial Reporting*

Interim reports should include financial statements (condensed or complete) for the following periods:

- Balance sheets as of the end of the current interim period and a comparative balance sheet as of the end of the immediately preceding financial year.

- Income statements for the current interim period and cumulatively for the current financial year to date, with comparative income statements for the comparable interim periods (current and year-to-date) of the immediately preceding financial year.

- A statement showing changes in equity cumulatively for the current financial year to date, with a comparative statement for the comparable year-to-date period of the immediately preceding financial year.

- A cash flow statement cumulatively for the current financial year to date, with a comparative statement for the comparable year-to-date period of the immediately preceding financial year.

If an entity's interim financial report is in compliance with IAS 34, that fact should be disclosed. An interim financial report may not be described as complying with IFRS unless it complies with all of the requirements of International Financial Reporting Standards.

Generally, the same accounting policies used in the latest annual financial statements should be applied in interim statements, except for accounting policy changes made after the date of the most recent annual financial statements that will be reflected in the next annual financial statements.

The frequency of interim reporting (annual, half-yearly, or quarterly) should not affect the measurement of annual results (i.e., measurements for interim reporting purposes should be made on a year-to-date basis, thus each interim period is considered part of the larger full financial year).

The principles for recognizing and measuring losses from inventory write-downs, restructurings, or impairments in an interim period should be the same as those that an entity would follow if only annual financial statements were prepared. However, if such items are recognized and measured in one interim period and the estimate changes in a subsequent interim period of that financial year, the original estimate should be changed in the subsequent interim period either by accrual of an additional amount of loss or by reversal of the previously recognized amount. Income tax expense recognized in each interim period should be based on the best estimate of the weighted average annual income tax rate expected for the full financial year. Amounts accrued for income tax expense in one interim period may have to be adjusted in a subsequent interim period of that financial year if the estimate of the annual income tax rate changes.

Revenues that are received seasonally, cyclically, or occasionally within a financial year should not be anticipated or deferred as of an interim date if anticipation or deferral would not be appropriate at the end of the year. Costs that are incurred unevenly during a year should be anticipated or deferred for interim reporting purposes if it is also appropriate to anticipate or defer that type of cost at the end of the year.

A change in accounting policy should be applied either retrospectively or, if it is not practicable to do so, prospectively from the beginning of the year.

# ¶ 2900. Leases

U.S. GAAP

## ¶ 2901. Main Authoritative Sources

- SFAS No. 13, *Accounting for Leases*
- SFAS No. 98, *Accounting for Leases*

## ¶ 2902. Lessees

A lease is considered a capital lease if, at inception, it meets one or more of the following criteria:

- The lease transfers ownership of the property to the lessee by the end of the lease term.
- The lease contains a bargain purchase option.
- The lease term is equal to 75% or more of the estimated economic life of the leased property. This criterion should not be used for purposes of classifying the lease, however, if the beginning of the lease term falls within the last 25% of the total estimated economic life of the leased property, including earlier years of use.
- The present value at the beginning of the lease term of the minimum lease payments, excluding that portion of the payments representing executory costs to be paid by the lessor, including any profit thereon, equals or exceeds 90% of the excess of the fair value of the leased property. This criterion should not be used for purposes of classifying the lease, however, if the beginning of the lease term falls within the last 25% of the total estimated economic life of the leased property, including earlier years of use.

Any lease that does not meet the criteria for a capital lease is accounted for as an operating lease. When accounting for an operating lease, the rented asset and the corresponding long-term liability are not recorded; instead, rent expense is debited periodically and cash (or a short-term accrued liability) is credited.

In accounting for a capital lease, the transaction is treated as if an asset was being acquired and a corresponding liability incurred. The asset and liability are recorded at the lower of:

- The present value of the minimum lease payments (excluding executing costs) over the lease term, or
- The fair market value of the asset at inception of the lease.

The present value of the minimum lease payments is computed using the lessee's incremental borrowing rate unless the implicit rate computed by the lessor is known and it is less than the lessee's incremental borrowing rate. Minimum lease payments comprise (1) payments that the lessee can be required or is expected to make during the lease term (other than amounts representing taxes, maintenance, insurance, and other executory costs included in the lease payments and paid by the lessor), plus

(2) any penalties that the lessee may pay for failure to renew or extend the lease beyond the lease term, plus (3) amounts that the lessee or a party related to the lessee guarantees to be realizable from the sale or release of the property at the end of the lease term.

The asset recorded is depreciated as follows:

- Over the estimated useful life of the asset (which may differ from the lease term) if the lease transfers ownership of the property to the lessee by the end of the lease term or the lease contains a bargain purchase option.

- Over the lease term if it is a capital lease because the lease term is equal to 75% or more of the estimated economic life of the leased property or the present value at the beginning of the lease term of the minimum lease payments equals or exceeds 90% of the excess of the fair value of the leased property.

In a capital lease transaction, the lessee is, in substance, financing the acquisition of the property. Lease payments are, therefore, essentially payments of principal and interest. Throughout the lease term, the effective interest method is used to allocate each lease payment between a reduction of the obligation and interest expense.

## ¶ 2903. Lessors

From the lessor's standpoint, a lease may be classified as one of the following types:

- Sales-type.
- Direct financing.
- Leveraged.
- Operating.

For a lease to be considered as other than an operating lease, it must meet any one of the aforementioned four criteria for a lease to be classified as a capital lease by the lessee. In addition, the lease must also meet both of the following conditions:

- The collectibility of the minimum lease payment is reasonably predictable.
- There are no important uncertainties as to the amount of un-reimbursable costs the lessor has yet to incur.

Leases that do not meet one of the first four and both of the last two criteria are considered operating leases. When a lease is classified as other than an operating lease, it is further classified as follows:

- Sales-type. If the lease results in a manufacturer's or dealer's profit or loss it is classified as a sales-type lease. Profit or loss is determined as the difference between the fair value of the leased property and its carrying value.

- Direct financing. If the lease is not a sales-type lease, it is considered a direct financing lease (i.e., the fair value of the leased property is equal to its carrying value, and no profit or loss arises).

- Leveraged. A leveraged lease (1) involves at least three parties, including lessee, a long-term lender, and lessor (investor), (2) has non-recourse financing provided by the long-term lender, (3) is a situation in which the lessor's net investment in the lease decreases during the early years of the lease and increases in the later years, and (4) would be classified as a direct financing lease if it were not a leveraged lease

Any lease that does not meet the foregoing criteria is accounted for as an operating lease (i.e., lease payments received or receivable are deemed rental income).

In accounting for a sales-type lease, the lessor records as sales revenue the present value of the minimum lease payments discounted at the interest rate implicit in the lease. Cost of sales equals the cost (or carrying value) of the leased property, reduced by the present value of any unguaranteed residual value. Initial direct costs are charged to operations when the sale is recognized. Unlike a sales-type lease, a direct financing lease does not result in a profit or loss from the asset; rather, any profit or loss is taken to income at a rate calculated to provide a constant rate of return on the net investment in the lease.

## ¶ 2904. Sale-Leaseback Transactions

Sale-leaseback transactions involve the sale of property by the owner and a lease of that property back to the seller. When the lease qualifies as a capital lease because it meets the required criteria, it should be accounted for as a capital lease; otherwise it should be accounted for as an operating lease. Any profit or loss on the sale (i.e., profit or loss that would be recognized if there were no leaseback) should be deferred and amortized into income in proportion to the depreciation of the leased asset (for a capital lease) or in proportion to the rental charged to expense over the lease term (for an operating lease). The following circumstances, however, result in exceptions to the general rule of profit or loss deferral:

- The seller-lessee relinquishes the right to substantially all of the remaining use of the property sold (retaining only a minor portion of such use), in which case the sale and the leaseback shall be accounted for as separate transactions based on their respective terms.

- The seller-lessee retains more than a minor part but less than substantially all of the use of the property through the leaseback and realizes a profit on the sale in excess of (1) the present value of the minimum lease payments over the lease term, if the leaseback is classified as an operating lease, or (2) the recorded amount of the leased asset, if the leaseback is classified as a capital lease.

- The fair value of the property at the time of the transaction is less than its un-depreciated cost, in which case a loss shall be recognized immediately up to the amount of the difference between un-depreciated cost and fair value.

The lessor in a sale-leaseback transaction (the purchaser) records the acquisition of the property and then accounts for the lease as a direct financing lease if the criteria are met; otherwise it is accounted for as an operating lease.

## ¶ 2905. Leases Involving Real Estate

There are four types of leases involving real estate:

- Land.
- Land and building.
- A portion of a building.
- Equipment and land.

From the lessee's standpoint, a lease involving only land is classified as a capital lease if the lease term is equal to 75% or more of the estimated economic life of the leased property or the present value at the beginning of the lease term of the minimum lease payments equals or exceeds 90% of the excess of the fair value of the leased property. From the lessor's standpoint, if either the lease transfers ownership of the property to the lessee by the end of the lease term or the lease contains a bargain purchase option *and* collectibility of the minimum lease payment is reasonably predictable and there are no important uncertainties as to the amount of un-reimbursable costs the lessor has yet to incur, the lease is classified as a sales-type or direct financing lease, whichever is appropriate; otherwise, the lease is considered an operating lease.

For a lease involving land and building, if either the lease transfers ownership of the property to the lessee by the end of the lease term or the lease contains a bargain purchase option, both the land and building components of the lease are classified as capital leases (but capitalized in separate accounts) by the lessee, with the present value of the minimum lease payments allocated between the two components based on their relative fair values. If neither of the foregoing criteria is met, however, and the value of the land is less than 25% of the total fair value, both the land and building are treated as a single unit. If the fair value of the land is 25% or more of the total fair value, the land and building elements should be accounted for separately. From the lessor's perspective, if either the lease transfers ownership of the property to the lessee by the end of the lease term or the lease contains a bargain purchase option *and* collectibility of the minimum lease payment is reasonably predictable and there are no important uncertainties as to the amount of un-reimbursable costs the lessor has yet to incur, the lease is treated as a single unit and classified as a sales-type or direct financing lease, whichever is appropriate; otherwise, the lease is considered an operating lease.

For a lease involving a portion of a building, if the fair value is reasonably determinable, the lease is classified by the lessee in the same manner as a lease involving land and building; if both the cost and the fair value are reasonably determinable, the lease is classified by the lessor in the same manner as a lease involving land and building. If neither the cost nor the fair value is not reasonably determinable, the lease is considered an operating lease.

For a lease that involves equipment and land, the components are considered separately both by the lessee and the lessor and allocated based on a reasonable and appropriate measure.

IFRS

# ¶ 2906. Main Authoritative Sources

- IAS 17, *Leases*

# ¶ 2907. Lessees

Under IFRS, a capital lease is referred to as a finance lease, which is a lease that transfers substantially all the risks and rewards incidental to ownership of an asset. Title may or may not eventually be transferred. Indicators that a lease is a finance lease include the following:

- The lease transfers ownership of the asset to the lessee by the end of the lease term.
- The lessee has the option to purchase the asset at a price that is expected to be sufficiently lower than the fair value at the date the option becomes exercisable.
- The lease term is for the major part of the economic life of the asset, even if title is not transferred.
- At the inception of the lease, the present value of the minimum lease payments amounts to at least substantially all of the fair value of the leased asset.
- The leased asset is of such a specialized nature that only the lessee can use it without major modifications.

Leases not qualifying as finance leases are operating leases. Lease payments under an operating lease are recognized as an expense on a straight-line basis over the lease term, unless another systematic basis is more representative of the time pattern of the user's benefit.

In accounting for a finance lease, an asset and corresponding liability are recognized at the commencement of the lease term at amounts equal to the lower of (1) fair value of the leased property or (2) the present value of the minimum lease payments. The discount rate to be used in calculating the present value of the minimum lease payments is the interest rate implicit in the lease, if this is practicable to determine; if not, the lessee's incremental borrowing rate should be used. Minimum lease payments comprise (1) the payments over the lease term the lessee is or can be required to make, excluding contingent rent, costs for services and taxes to be paid by and reimbursed to the lessor, plus (2) any amounts guaranteed by the lessee or by a party related to the lessee.

The recognized lease asset should be depreciated in a manner consistent with depreciable assets owned; if there is no reasonable certainty that the lessee will obtain ownership by the end of the lease term, the asset should be depreciated over the shorter of the lease term or its useful life. Minimum lease payments should be apportioned between the finance charge (i.e., interest) and the reduction of the outstanding liability in a manner that yields a constant periodic rate of interest on the remaining balance of the liability.

## ¶ 2908. Lessors

From the lessor's standpoint, leases are also classified either as finance or operating leases. Under a finance lease, a receivable is recognized for the net investment in the lease, which represents the gross investment (i.e., the aggregate of minimum lease payments receivable plus any unguaranteed residual value of the asset) discounted (at the rate implicit in the lease) to its present value. Finance income should be based on a pattern reflecting a constant periodic rate of return on the lessor's net investment in the lease.

Manufacturer or dealer lessors should recognize selling profit or loss in the period in accordance with the entity's policies for outright sales. The sales revenue recognized at the commencement of the lease term by a manufacturer or dealer lessor is the lower of (1) fair value of the asset, or (2) the present value of the minimum lease by applying a market rate of interest. The cost of sale recognized is the cost (or carrying amount, if different) of the leased property, less the present value of the unguaranteed residual value.

A lease not qualifying as a finance lease is an operating lease for which income is recognized on a straight-line basis over the lease term, unless another systematic basis is more representative of the time pattern in which use benefit derived from the leased asset is diminished.

## ¶ 2909. Sale-Leaseback Transactions

A sale-leaseback transaction involves the sale of an asset and the leasing back of the same asset. If a sale-leaseback transaction results in a finance lease, any excess of sales proceeds over the carrying amount of the asset should be deferred and amortized over the lease term. If a sale-leaseback transaction results in an operating lease, and it is clear that the transaction is established at fair value, any profit or loss should be recognized immediately. If the sale price is below fair value, any profit or loss should be recognized immediately except that, if the loss will be compensated for by future lease payments at below market price, any profit or loss should be deferred and amortized in proportion to the lease payments over the period for which the asset is expected to be used. If the sale price is above fair value, the excess over fair value should be deferred and amortized over the period for which the asset is expected to be used.

The lessor in a sale-leaseback transaction (the purchaser) records the acquisition of the property and then accounts for the lease as a finance lease (if the criteria are met) or as an operating lease.

## ¶ 2910. Leases Involving Real Estate

Leases of land and of buildings should be classified as operating or finance leases in the same way as leases of other assets. Land and buildings elements of a lease should be considered separately for the purposes of lease classification. If title to both elements is expected to pass to the lessee by the end of the lease term, both should be classified as a finance lease, unless it is clear that the lease does not transfer substantially all risks and rewards incidental to ownership of one or both elements. When the land has an indefinite economic life, the land element is normally classified as an operating lease unless title is expected to pass to the lessee by the end of the lease term.

When classifying a lease of land and buildings, the minimum lease payments should be allocated between the land and the buildings elements in proportion to the relative fair values of the leasehold interests in the land element and buildings element of the lease at the inception of the lease. If the lease payments cannot be allocated reliably between these two elements, the entire lease should be classified as a finance lease, unless it is clear that both elements are operating leases, in which case the entire lease should be classified as an operating lease.

# ¶ 3000. Nonmonetary Transactions
## U.S. GAAP

## ¶ 3001. Main Authoritative Sources

- APB Opinion No. 29, *Accounting for Nonmonetary Transactions*
- FASB Interpretation No. 30, *Accounting for Involuntary Conversions of Nonmonetary Assets to Monetary Assets*

Accounting for nonmonetary transactions should be based on the fair values of assets or services involved. The basic principle is that cost of a nonmonetary asset acquired in exchange for another nonmonetary asset is the fair value of the asset surrendered or received, whichever is more clearly evident, with any gain or loss thereon recognized in earnings. Similarly, a nonmonetary asset received in a nonreciprocal transfer should be recorded at its fair value. A transfer of a nonmonetary asset to a stockholder or to another company in a nonreciprocal transfer should be recorded at the fair value of the asset transferred, and a gain or loss on the disposition should be recognized.

A nonmonetary exchange should be measured based on the recorded amount of an asset (i.e., a modification of the basic principle) if:

- Fair value cannot be determined within reasonable limits (i.e., there are major uncertainties regarding the realization of an assigned fair value).

- The transaction is an exchange of a product or property held for sale in the ordinary course of business for a product or property to be sold in the same line of business to facilitate sales to customers (other than the parties to the exchange).

- The exchange transaction lacks commercial substance.

A nonmonetary exchange is deemed to have commercial substance if (1) the risk, timing, or amount of the entity's future cash flows is expected to differ significantly from any of those of the transferred asset, or (2) the entity-specific value of the asset received differs from such value of the asset transferred and the difference is significant in relation to the fair values of the exchanged assets. If either condition is met, the transaction is considered to have commercial substance and thus should be accounted for at fair value; otherwise, the transaction should be accounted for based on the recorded amount of the asset relinquished (appropriately reduced for any indicated impairment). An asset's entity-specific value is its expected value in use by the entity, rather than the use that would be assumed generally by marketplace participants at large.

For exchanges involving monetary consideration (boot), the recipient of the boot has realized a gain on the exchange to the extent that the boot exceeds a proportionate share of the book value of the asset surrendered. The portion of the cost applicable to the realized amount is based on the ratio of the boot to the total consideration received (cash plus the fair value of the nonmonetary asset received) or, if more clearly evident, to the fair value of the nonmonetary asset transferred.

The payor of the boot should not recognize any gain; rather, the payor should record the asset received at the amount of the boot paid plus the recorded amount of the nonmonetary asset given up. If a loss results to either party, however, the full amount of the loss should be recorded. Note that an exchange of nonmonetary assets that would otherwise be based on recorded amounts but includes boot of 25% or more than the fair value of the exchange should be considered a monetary exchange and accounted for at fair values.

Involuntary conversions of nonmonetary assets to monetary assets are considered monetary transactions for which a gain or loss should be recognized even though a company reinvests or is obligated to reinvest the monetary assets to replace the nonmonetary assets. The gain or loss on involuntary conversion is the difference between the book value of the nonmonetary asset and the amount of monetary assets received.

IFRS

## ¶ 3002. Main Authoritative Sources

- IAS 16, *Property, Plant and Equipment*
- IAS 18, *Revenue*
- IAS 38, *Intangible Assets*

Although IFRS does not define the term "nonmonetary transaction," the basic principles in respect of exchanges of goods or services are (1) the exchange or swap of goods or services for those of a similar nature and value does not give rise to revenue, and (2) when goods are sold or services are rendered in exchange for dissimilar goods or services, the exchange is regarded as a transaction that does generate revenue, which should be measured at the fair value of the goods or services received, adjusted by the amount of any cash or cash equivalents transferred; when the fair value of the goods or services received cannot be measured reliably, revenue is measured at the fair value of the goods or services given up, adjusted by the amount of any cash or cash equivalents transferred.

Note, however, that in respect of exchanges of property, plant and equipment or exchanges of intangible assets, the acquired item is measured at fair value unless (1) the exchange transaction lacks commercial substance, or (2) the fair value of neither the asset received nor the asset given up is reliably measurable; if the acquired item is not measured at fair value, its cost is measured at the carrying amount of the asset given up.

An exchange transaction has commercial substance if:

- The configuration (risk, timing, and amount) of the cash flows of the asset received differs from the configuration of the cash flows of the asset transferred.
- The entity-specific value of the portion of the entity's operations affected by the transaction (i.e., after-tax cash flows) changes as a result of the exchange and the difference is significant relative to the fair value of the assets exchanged.

# ¶ 3100. Pension Benefits

## U.S. GAAP

## ¶ 3101. Main Authoritative Sources

- SFAS No. 87, *Employers' Accounting for Pensions*
- SFAS No. 88, *Employers' Accounting for Settlements and Curtailments of Defined Benefit Pension Plans and for Termination Benefits*

## ¶ 3102. Pension Costs

Pension expense each year under a defined contribution plan is generally equal to the amount of cash contribution called for by the plan. However, if a plan requires contributions to be made after an employee retires or terminates, the estimated cost of such postemployment contributions should be recognized during the employee's service period.

Periodic pension expense for a defined benefit plan consists of the following five basic components:

- *Service cost*, which is the actuarial present value of pension benefits earned by employees during the period.
- *Interest cost*, which represents the increase in the present value of the pension obligation using an assumed discount rate.
- *Actual return on plan assets*, which is the difference between the fair values of plan assets at the beginning and end of the period, adjusted for contributions and benefit payments.
- *Amortization of prior service cost or credit included in other comprehensive income* represents amortization of the cost of pension benefits granted retroactively either at the plan initiation date or by plan amendment.
- *Gains or losses* are changes in either the benefit obligation or in the value of plan assets resulting from experience different from that assumed of from changes in actuarial assumptions.

The gain or loss component is reflected in the measurement of plan assets and PBO. Gains and losses are expected to even out over a period of time, so the amount of cumulative (unrecognized) gain or loss need not be amortized and included in periodic pension expense unless it exceeds a defined threshold amount (referred to as the corridor approach). The threshold amount is 10% of the larger of pension obligation at the beginning of the year or the market related value of plan assets at the beginning of the year. Gains and losses not immediately recognized in periodic pension expense must be recognized as increases or decreases in other comprehensive income.

The funded status of a single-employer benefit plan should be recognized in the balance sheet as an asset or liability (as applicable). Funded status is measured as the difference between the fair value of plan assets and the pension obligation (i.e., the actuarial present value of the projected pension benefits that are attributable to employment as of a specific date). When more than one plan exists, the status of each individual overfunded plan should be aggregated and recognized as an asset; the status of each underfunded plan should be similarly aggregated and recognized as a liability

Generally, the measurement date for plan assets and liabilities must be as of the balance sheet date. In selecting the discount rate to measure the pension obligation, the reference should be to rates of return on high-quality fixed income investments. The objective of using that approach is to measure the single amount that, if invested at the measurement date in a portfolio of high-quality debt instruments, would provide the necessary future cash flows to pay benefits when they become due. In other than a zero coupon portfolio, assumed discount rates should take into account expected future reinvestment rates, which should be extrapolated from the yield curve at the measurement date. Note that assumed discount rates must be re-evaluated at each measurement date to give effect to changes in the general level of interest rates.

Employers with two or more plans should account for each plan separately. Unless an employer clearly has the right to use assets of one plan to pay benefits of another, any liability to be recognized for one plan may not be reduced because another plan has assets in excess of its pension obligation.

## ¶ 3103. Settlements and Curtailments

A settlement is defined as a transaction that:

- Is irrevocable.
- Relieves the employer (or the plan) of primary responsibility for a pension benefit obligation.
- Eliminates significant risks related to the obligation and the assets used to effect the settlement.

A curtailment is an event that significantly reduces the expected years of future service of present employees or eliminates for a significant number of employees the accrual of defined benefits for some or all of their future services. Curtailments include:

- Termination of employees' services earlier than expected.
- Termination or suspension of a plan so that employees do not earn additional defined benefits for future services.

If the entire pension obligation is settled, the maximum gain or loss is reported in the settlement period. If only a portion of the obligation is settled, however, only that portion of the gain or loss is recognized currently. The maximum amount of gain or loss to be reported is the net gain or loss remaining in accumulated other comprehensive income existing at the date of settlement. If the cost of all settlements in a year is less than or equal to the sum of the service and interest cost components, gain or loss is permitted (but not required) for these settlements.

A curtailment will affect some portion of unrecognized pension cost components, such as unrecognized prior service cost, and net gain or loss in accumulated other comprehensive income. If the net effect of the curtailment is a loss, the loss should be recognized when it is probable that the curtailment will occur and the effects are reasonably estimable. If a gain results, it should be recognized when the affected employees terminate or when the plan suspension or amendment is adopted by the company.

IFRS

## ¶ 3104. Main Authoritative Sources

- IAS 19, *Employee Benefits*

## ¶ 3105. Pension Costs

In a defined contribution plan, a liability (i.e., accrued contribution payable) should be recognized, together with a corresponding expense. For a defined benefit plan, the amount charged to profit or loss during the period comprises the following elements:

- *Current service cost*, which is the actuarial present value of benefits attributed to employee services rendered during the period.

- *Interest cost*, which represents the increase in present value of the benefit obligation.

- *The expected return on plan assets*, which is the anticipated return at the beginning of the period, based on market expectations.

- *Actuarial gains and losses*, which is the difference between previous actuarial assumptions and actual experience.

- *Past service cost*, which is the increase in present value of the benefit obligation for employee service in prior periods following the introduction of or changes to the plan.

- *The effects of any curtailments or settlements*; a settlement occurs when the entity enters into a transaction that eliminates all further legal or constructive obligation for part or all of the benefits provided under the plan; a curtailment occurs when either (1) the entity is committed to making a material reduction in the number of employees covered by a plan, or (2) the entity amends the terms of the plan so that a material element of future service by current employees will no longer qualify for benefits (or will qualify only for reduced benefits).

Actuarial gains or losses are reflected in annual expense (i.e., the amount charged to profit or loss) if they exceed a threshold amount (referred to as the corridor approach). The amount included in expense is the greater of (1) 10% of the present value of the benefit obligation, and (2) 10% of the fair value of any plan assets, both determined at the end of the previous period. Past service cost should be recognized as an expense on a straight-line basis over the average period remaining until the benefits become vested; to the extent that the benefits vest immediately, past service cost should be immediately recognized in profit or loss.

The amount recognized as a defined benefit liability is the net of the following items:

- The present value of the benefit obligation at the balance sheet date.
- Any actuarial gains (less any actuarial losses) not recognized.
- Any past service cost not yet recognized.
- The fair value at the balance sheet date of plan assets (if any.)

If the calculation results in a defined benefit asset, such asset may not be recognized in an amount that exceeds the lower of (1) any cumulative unrecognized net actuarial losses and past service cost, or (2) the present value of any economic benefits available in the form of refunds from the plan or reductions in future contributions to the plan. Note that the difference between the amount of the asset calculated and recognized should be included in annual expense.

The present value of the benefit obligation and of the fair value of any plan assets should be determined with sufficient regularity so that the amounts recognized do not differ materially from the amounts that would be determined at the balance sheet date.

## ¶ 3106. Settlements and Curtailments

As discussed above, gains or losses on the settlement or curtailment of a defined benefit plan should be recognized in profit or loss when the settlement or curtailment occurs. The amount of any gain or loss is computed as the net amount of the following components:

- Any resulting change in the present value of the benefit obligation.
- Any resulting change in the fair value of the plan assets.
- Any related actuarial gains and losses and past service cost not previously recognized.

# ¶ 3200. Postretirement, Postemployment, and Other Employee Benefits

## U.S. GAAP

## ¶ 3201. Main Authoritative Sources

- SFAS No. 106, *Employers' Accounting for Postretirement Benefits Other Than Pensions*
- SFAS No. 112, *Employers' Accounting for Postretirement Benefits*
- SFAS No. 43, *Accounting for Compensated Absences*
- SFAS No. 5, *Accounting for Contingencies*

## ¶ 3202. Postretirement Benefits Other than Pensions

Postretirement benefits (other than pensions) are benefits expected to be provided by an employer to current and former employees, their beneficiaries, and covered dependents. Although SFAS No. 112, *Employers' Accounting for Postemployment Benefits*, applies to all such benefits, its focus is on health care benefits.

In general, annual other postretirement benefit expense (referred to as benefit expense) for a defined contribution plan is equal to the aggregate amount of contributions made to all individual accounts of plan participants for periods in which individuals render services.

In order to compute annual benefit expense for a defined benefit plan, two obligations must be determined: (1) EPBO; and (2) APBO. EPBO is the present value of benefits expected to be paid to employees, their beneficiaries, and covered dependents. Prior to the date on which employees become fully eligible for benefits, APBO simply represents the portion of EPBO attributable to services already rendered. At the full eligibility date, however, EPBO and APBO become equal in amount.

Benefit expense for a defined benefit plan comprises the following components:

- *Service cost*, which is the actuarial present value of postretirement benefits earned by employees in the current period.

- *Interest cost*, which represents the increase in the present value of accumulated postretirement benefit obligation attributable to the passage of time.

- *Actual return on plan assets* is the difference in fair values of plan assets (for a funded) plan at the beginning and end of the period, adjusted for contributions and benefit payments. If no formal funded *plan* exists (i.e., the employer, not a plan, holds assets that may be used to satisfy the benefit obligation), this component will not be a part of annual benefit expense.

- *Amortization of prior service cost included in accumulated other comprehensive income* is amortization of the cost of benefits granted retroactively either by amendment or upon initiation of the plan.

- *Gains or losses* are changes in either the benefit obligation or in the value of plan assets resulting from experience different from that assumed or from changes in actuarial assumptions.

The amount of cumulative (unrecognized) gain or loss need not be amortized and included in periodic benefit expense, unless it exceeds a defined threshold amount (referred to as the corridor approach). The threshold amount is 10% of the larger of APBO at the beginning of the year or the market related value of plan assets at the beginning of the year.

The funded status of a single-employer benefit plan (measured as the difference between the fair value of plan assets and the APBO) should be recognized in the balance sheet as an asset or liability (as applicable). When more than one plan exists, the status of each individual overfunded plan should be aggregated and recognized as an asset; the status of each underfunded plan should be similarly aggregated and recognized as a liability.

In general, the measurement date for plan assets and liabilities must be as of the balance sheet date. In selecting the discount rate to measure the APBO, the reference should be to rates of return on high-quality fixed income investments. The objective of using that approach is to measure the single amount that, if invested at the measurement date in a portfolio of high-quality debt instruments, would provide the necessary future cash flows to pay benefits when they become due. In other than a zero coupon portfolio, assumed discount rates should take into account expected future reinvestment rates, which should be extrapolated from the yield curve at the measurement date. Note that assumed discount rates must be re-evaluated at each measurement date to give effect to changes in the general level of interest rates.

Data from all unfunded plans may be aggregated for measurement purposes only if those plans provide different benefits to the same group of employees or those plans provide the same benefits to different groups of employees. Note, however, that an unfunded plan with plan assets must be measured separately.

## ¶ 3203. Settlements and Curtailments

A settlement of a defined benefit plan is a transaction that:

- Is irrevocable.
- Relieves the employer (or the plan) of primary responsibility for a pension benefit obligation.
- Eliminates significant risks related to the obligation and the assets used to effect the settlement.

A curtailment is an event that significantly reduces the expected years of future service of present employees or eliminates for a significant number of employees the accrual of defined benefits for some or all of their future services. Curtailments include:

- Termination of employees' services earlier than expected.

- Termination or suspension of a plan so that employees do not earn additional defined benefits for future services.

The maximum gain or loss that can be recognized in income in a settlement transaction is the remaining gain or loss included in accumulated other comprehensive income. If a net curtailment loss occurs, it should be recognized in income only when it is probable that the curtailment will take place and the amount is reasonably estimable. If a net curtailment gain arises, it is recognized in income when the related employees are terminated or the plan suspension or amendment is adopted.

## ¶ 3204. Postemployment and Other Benefits

Postemployment benefits are all types of benefits (including compensated absences) provided to former or inactive employees (before retirement), their beneficiaries, and covered dependents. A company must accrue a liability for postemployment benefits if all of the following conditions are met:

- The company's obligation is attributable to services already rendered by employees.

- The obligation relates to rights that vest (i.e., rights that are not contingent on an employee's future service) or accumulate.

- Payment of the compensation is probable.

- The amount can be reasonably estimated.

Note that U.S. GAAP does not address the manner in which the amount of the postemployment liability should be determined. Measurement issues, such as whether the liability should be based on current or future pay rates, whether the liability should be discounted, and when the effect of scheduled increases should be accrued, are not discussed.

Postemployment benefits that do not meet the conditions for accrual should be accounted for as a loss contingency, which also requires a liability to be recognized when (1) information available prior to issuance of the financial statements indicates that it is probable that a liability had been incurred at the date of the financial statements, and (2) the amount of loss can be reasonably estimated.

IFRS

## ¶ 3205. Main Authoritative Sources

- IAS 19, *Employee Benefits*

**Note:** IAS 19 does not distinguish between types of postretirement benefits (i.e., pensions and others) or between postretirement and postemployment benefits. The following discussion is identical to that of pension benefits; it is included here to facilitate comparison to the requirements of U.S. GAAP.

## ¶ 3206. Postretirement Benefits Other than Pensions

In a defined contribution plan, a liability (i.e., accrued contribution payable) should be recognized, together with a corresponding expense. For a defined benefit plan, the amount charged to profit or loss during the period comprises the following elements:

- *Current service cost*, which is the actuarial present value of benefits attributed to employee services rendered during the period.
- *Interest cost*, which represents the increase in present value of the benefit obligation.
- *The expected return on plan assets*, which is the anticipated return at the beginning of the period, based on market expectations.
- *Actuarial gains and losses*, which is the difference between previous actuarial assumptions and actual experience.
- *Past service cost*, which is the increase in present value of the benefit obligation for employee service in prior periods following the introduction of or changes to the plan.
- *The effects of any curtailments or settlements*; a settlement occurs when the entity enters into a transaction that eliminates all further legal or constructive obligation for part or all of the benefits provided under the plan; a curtailment occurs when either (1) the entity is committed to making a material reduction in the number of employees covered by a plan, or (2) the entity amends the terms of the plan so that a material element of future service by current employees will no longer qualify for benefits (or will qualify only for reduced benefits).

Actuarial gains or losses are reflected in annual expense (i.e., the amount charged to profit or loss) if they exceed a threshold amount (referred to as the corridor approach). The amount included in expense is the greater of (1) 10% of the present value of the benefit obligation, and (2) 10% of the fair value of any plan assets, both determined at the end of the previous period. Past service cost should be recognized as an expense on a straight-line basis over the average period remaining until the benefits become vested; to the extent that the benefits vest immediately, past service cost should be immediately recognized in profit or loss.

The amount recognized as a defined benefit liability is the net of the following items:

- The present value of the benefit obligation at the balance sheet date.
- Any actuarial gains (less any actuarial losses) not recognized.
- Any past service cost not yet recognized.
- The fair value at the balance sheet date of plan assets (if any).

If the calculation results in a defined benefit asset, such asset may not be recognized in an amount that exceeds the lower of (1) any cumulative unrecognized net actuarial losses and past service cost, or (2) the present value of any economic benefits available in the form of refunds from the plan or reductions in future contributions to the plan. Note that the difference between the amount of the asset calculated and recognized should be included in annual expense.

The present value of the benefit obligation and of the fair value of any plan assets should be determined with sufficient regularity so that the amounts recognized do not differ materially from the amounts that would be determined at the balance sheet date.

## ¶ 3207. Settlements and Curtailments

Gains or losses on the settlement or curtailment of a defined benefit plan should be recognized in profit or loss when the settlement or curtailment occurs. The amount of any gain or loss is computed as the net amount of the following components:

- Any resulting change in the present value of the benefit obligation.
- Any resulting change in the fair value of the plan assets.
- Any related actuarial gains and losses and past service cost not previously recognized.

## ¶ 3208. Postemployment and Other Benefits

For short-term employee benefits, when an employee has already rendered service to an entity during an accounting period, the entity should recognize the undiscounted amount of the benefits expected to be paid in exchange for such service.

Specifically, in respect of compensated absences, the cost of such absences should be recognized as follows:

- For accumulating compensated absences, when employees render service that increases their entitlement to future compensated absences.
- For non-accumulating compensated absences, when the absences occur.

# ¶ 3300. Related Party Transactions

U.S. GAAP

## ¶ 3301. Main Authoritative Sources

- SFAS No. 57, *Related Party Disclosures*

In general, the following are considered to be related parties:

- Affiliates.
- Investees accounted for by the equity method (including those of investments otherwise to be accounted for under the equity method but for the election to account for such investments at fair value).
- Trusts (e.g., pension or profit-sharing trusts managed or under the trusteeship of management) for the benefit of employees.
- Principal owners of the company.
- Management of the company.
- Members of the immediate family of principal owners or management.
- Any party with which the company may do business if either party to the transaction does or can control or significantly influence the management or operating policies of the other party to an extent that either party might be prevented from pursuing its own interests.
- Any party that can significantly influence the management or operating policies of other parties to a transaction, or that has an equity interest in one of the transacting parties and can significantly influence the other party to an extent that either of the transacting parties might be prevented from pursuing its own interests.

There is a general presumption that transactions (including unrecorded transactions) between related parties cannot be carried out on an arm's-length basis. Accordingly, information about such transactions should not imply that they are consummated on terms that are equivalent to those that prevail in arm's-length transactions unless that assertion can be substantiated.

The following disclosures are required for all related-party transactions:

- The nature of the relationship(s).
- A description of the transactions (including transactions to which no amounts or nominal amounts were ascribed).
- Any other information deemed necessary for an understanding of the effects of the transactions on the financial statements.
- The dollar amounts of transactions and the effects of any change in the method of establishing the terms from that used in the preceding period.
- Amounts due to or from related parties and the terms and manner of settlement (including amounts due from officers and employees).

- The nature of common control (e.g., two companies with a common parent) with another company even when no business is transacted between them, if the possibility that the mere existence of such common control may result in operating results or financial position significantly different from those that would have been obtained had the companies been autonomous (for example, when two companies in the same line of business are controlled by a parent with the ability to influence the volume of business done by each).

IFRS

## ¶ 3302. Main Authoritative Sources

- IAS 24, *Related Party Disclosures*

A party is deemed a related party to an entity if:

- Directly, or indirectly through one or more intermediaries, the party (1) controls, is controlled by, or is under common control with, the entity, (2) has an interest in the entity that gives it significant influence over the entity, or (3) has joint control over the entity.
- The party is an associate of the entity.
- The party is a joint venture in which the entity is a venturer.
- The party is a member of the key management personnel of the entity or its parent.
- The party is a post-employment benefit plan for the benefit of employees of the entity, or of any entity that is a related party of the entity.

Note that a related party includes a close member of individuals, who, themselves, qualify as related parties.

A related party transaction represents a transfer of resources, services or obligations between related parties, regardless of whether a price is charged.

Relationships between parents and subsidiaries should be disclosed irrespective of whether there have been transactions between them. Disclosure should include the name of the entity's parent and, if different, the ultimate controlling party. If neither the entity's parent nor the ultimate controlling party produces financial statements available for public use, the name of the next most senior parent that does publish such financial statements should also be disclosed. In addition, if there have been transactions between related parties, disclosure should be made of the nature of the relationship as well as information about the transactions and outstanding balances necessary for an understanding of the potential effect of the relationship on the financial statements. Such disclosure should be made separately for each of the following categories:

- The parent.
- Entities with joint control or significant influence over the entity.
- Subsidiaries.
- Associates.

- Joint ventures in which the entity is a venturer.
- Key management personnel of the entity or its parent.
- Other related parties.

Compensation of key management personnel for each of the following categories (and in total) should be disclosed:

- Short-term employee benefits.
- Post-employment benefits.
- Other long-term benefits.
- Termination benefits.
- Share-based payment.

Key management personnel are individuals having authority and responsibility for planning, directing, and controlling the activities of the entity (directly or indirectly), including (executive and non-executive) directors of the entity.

# ¶ 3400. Reporting in Hyperinflationary Economies

### U.S. GAAP

## ¶ 3401. Main Authoritative Sources

- SFAS No. 89, *Financial Reporting and Changing Prices*

Companies are permitted (but not required) to provide supplementary information about the effects of changing prices. In the broad sense, there are two types of accounting for changing prices: (1) accounting for changes in the general prices of all goods and services (constant dollar accounting); and (2) accounting for specific changes related to identified accounts (current cost accounting).

Constant dollar accounting requires that the Consumer Price Index for all urban consumers (CPIU) be used to measure the change in the general purchasing power of the dollar. The minimum supplemental information to be provided is:

- Information on income from continuing operations for the current year.
- Purchasing power gain or loss on net monetary items for the current year.

The minimum information required to be disclosed in connection with current cost accounting is:

- Information on income from continuing operations for the current year.
- Current cost amounts of inventory, and property, plant, and equipment (PP&E) at the end of the current year; for inventory, current cost is the current purchase price or manufacturing cost, and for property, current cost is the current cost of acquiring the same service potential of the asset. Depreciation expense is measured on the basis of average current cost during the period of use.
- Increases or decreases for the current year in the current cost amounts of inventory, and PP&E, net of inflation.

As in the case of constant dollar accounting, a comprehensive restatement of all balance-sheet and income statement accounts is permitted.

In addition to the information required in constant dollars and in current costs for the current year, the following information must be provided for the five latest years:

- Net sales and other operating revenues.
- Historical costs/constant dollar information for (1) income from continuing operations, (2) earnings per share from continuing operations, and (3) net assets at the end of each year.
- Increases or decreases in the current cost amounts of inventory, and PP&E, net of inflation.
- Purchasing power gain or loss on net monetary items.
- Cash dividends per common share.

- Market price per common share at the end of each year.
- CPIU used (average or end-of-year) in measuring income from continuing operations on a constant dollar basis.

Each amount in the five-year summary is to be stated in the same constant dollars. Accordingly, the amounts may be based on one of the following:

- Latest year average-for-the-year or current end-of-year dollars (whichever was used to measure income from continuing operations on a constant dollar basis).
- Dollars of the base year (1967) used by the Bureau of Labor in calculating CPIU.
- CPIU used (average or end-of-year) in measuring income from continuing operations on a constant dollar basis.

IFRS

# ¶ 3402. Main Authoritative Sources

- IAS 29, *Financial Reporting in Hyperinflationary Economies*

Financial statements of an entity operating in a hyperinflationary economy should be restated in terms of the measuring unit current at the balance sheet date. Hyperinflation is indicated by the following characteristics of the economic environment of a country:

- The general population prefers to keep its wealth in nonmonetary assets or in a relatively stable foreign currency.
- Amounts of local currency held are immediately invested to maintain purchasing power.
- The general population regards monetary amounts in terms of a relatively stable foreign currency (rather than of the local currency).
- Sales and purchases on credit take place at prices that compensate for the expected loss of purchasing power during the credit period.
- Interest rates, wages and prices are linked to a price index.
- The cumulative inflation rate over three years is approaching or exceeds 100%.

The restatement of historical financial statements is accomplished as follows:

- Balance sheet items not already stated at current cost (i.e., monetary assets and liabilities) should be restated by applying a general price index.
- Income statement items are restated by applying the change in the general price index from the dates on which the items were initially recorded.
- Gain or loss on the net monetary position (which may be estimated by applying the price index change to the weighted average net monetary position for the period) should be included in profit and loss.

In current cost financial statements, balance sheet items already stated at current cost should not be restated because they are already expressed in terms of the measuring unit current at the reporting date. In the current cost income statement, all amounts must be restated into the measuring unit current at the balance sheet date by applying a general price index, because cost of sales and depreciation are recorded at current costs at the time of consumption, and sales and other expenses are recorded at their money amounts when the transactions occurred.

When an economy ceases to be hyperinflationary (and thus restatement of the current period's financial statements is not necessary) amounts expressed in the measuring unit current at the end of the previous reporting period are deemed to be the basis for the carrying amounts in subsequent financial statements.

# ¶ 3500. Segmental Reporting
U.S. GAAP

## ¶ 3501. Main Authoritative Sources

- SFAS No. 131, *Disclosures about Segments of an Enterprise and Related Information*

An operating segment is a component of an entity:

- That engages in business activities from which it earns revenues and incurs expenses (including revenues and expenses relating to transactions with other components of the same enterprise).

- Whose operating results are regularly reviewed by the enterprise's chief operating decision-maker (CODM) to assess the performance of the individual segment and make decisions about resources to be allocated to the segment.

- For which discrete financial information is available and is generated by or based on the internal financial reporting system.

The term "chief operating decision-maker" identifies a function, not necessarily a manager with a specific title. That function is to allocate resources to and assess the performance of the segments of an enterprise. Often the CODM of an enterprise is its chief executive officer or chief operating officer, but it may be a group of individuals.

A reportable segment (i.e., one for which information is required to be disclosed) is one that:

- Has been identified as an operating segment (or has been aggregated with one or more other operating segments).

- Exceeds specific quantitative thresholds.

Two or more operating segments may be aggregated if the segments have similar economic characteristics, and if the segments are similar in each of the following areas:

- The nature of the products and services.
- The nature of the production processes.
- The type or class of customer for their products and services.
- The methods used to distribute their products or provide their services.
- If applicable, the nature of the regulatory environment (e.g., banking, insurance, or public utilities).

Separate disclosure of information is required about an operating segment (or aggregation of segments) that meets any of the following thresholds:

- Its reported revenue, including both sales to external customers and inter-segment sales or transfers, is 10% or more of the combined internal and external revenue of all reported operating segments.

- The absolute amount of its reported profit or loss is 10% or more of the greater, in absolute amount, of (1) the combined reported profit of all operating segments that did not report a loss, or (2) the combined reported loss of all operating segments that did report a loss.
- Its assets are 10% or more of the combined assets of all operating segments.

If the total of external revenue by operating segments constitutes less than 75% of the total consolidated revenue, additional operating segments must be identified as reportable segments (even if they do not meet the quantitative thresholds) until at least 75% of the total consolidated revenue is included in reportable segments. Information about non-reportable segments and other business activities should be combined in a category described as "all other."

For each reportable segment, the following annual information is required to be disclosed for each period for which an income statement is presented:

- Factors used to identify reportable segments, including the basis of organization (e.g., differences in products and services, geographic areas, regulatory environments, or a combination of factors).
- Types of products and services from which each operating segment derives its revenues.
- Profit or loss.
- Revenues from transactions with external customers.
- Revenues from transactions with other operating segments.
- Interest income.
- Interest expense.
- Depreciation, depletion, and amortization expense.
- Extraordinary and unusual items.
- Equity in the net income of investees accounted for by the equity method.
- Income tax expense or benefit.
- Significant non-cash items (other than depreciation, amortization, and depletion).
- Total assets.

In addition to the foregoing data, reconciliations of the following to corresponding amounts on the entity's (consolidated) financial statements are required for the aggregate of all segments:

- Revenue.
- Profit or loss.
- Total assets.
- Every other significant item.

The following information is required to be disclosed in condensed interim financial statements:

- Revenues from external customers for each operating segment.
- Inter-segment revenues for each operating segment.
- Segment profit or loss for each operating segment.
- A reconciliation of the total of the operating segments' profits or losses to consolidated income or loss.
- Total assets for each operating segment for which there has been a material change from the amount disclosed in the last annual report.

Additionally, the following information is required on an entity-wide basis unless it is disclosed as part of the information about reportable segments:

- Revenues from external customers for each product and service or each group of similar products and services unless it is impracticable to do so.
- The following geographic amounts based on information used to produce the general-purpose financial statements, unless it is impracticable to do so:

  — Revenues from external customers (1) attributed to the enterprise's country of domicile, and (2) in each country from which the operating segment derives significant revenues.

  — Long-lived segment assets located (1) in the enterprise's country of domicile, and (2) in each country in which the segment holds significant assets.

Disclosure is also required of the fact of reliance on a single external customer (including as a single customer a federal, state, or local government) from which 10% or more of revenues are derived and the amount of revenue earned from each such single customer.

IFRS

## ¶ 3502. Main Authoritative Sources

- IAS 14, *Segment Reporting*
- IFRS 8, *Operating Segments*

**Note:** Effective from January 1, 2009, IFRS 8 will replace IAS 14, which will be withdrawn (though early application of IFRS 8 is permitted). The discussions in this section include (1) the requirements of IAS 14, (2) followed by the requirements of IFRS 8.

## ¶ 3503. Under the Provisions of IAS 14

Entities having publicly traded debt or equity securities must report information both by business segments and geographical segments, with one designated as the primary basis and the other as the secondary basis. A business segment is defined as a distinguishable component of an entity that is engaged in providing an individual product or service (or a group of related products or services) and that is subject to risks and returns that are different from those of other business segments. A geographical segment is a distinguishable component of an entity engaged in providing products or services within a particular economic environment and that is subject to risks and returns that are different from those of components operating in other economic environments.

Whether an entity's primary segment reporting format is based on business or geographical segments is governed by the dominant source and nature of the entity's risks and returns (i.e., products or services or its operations in different countries). Determination of a business or geographical segment is, for most entities, based on organizational units for which information is reported to key management personnel or the senior operating decision maker.

A business segment or geographical segment is deemed a reportable segment if a majority of its revenue is earned from sales to external customers and (1) its revenue from sales to external customers and from transactions with other segments is 10% or more of the total revenue of all segments, or (2) its profit or loss is 10% or more of the combined result of all profitable segments or the combined result of all segments in a loss position, whichever is the greater in absolute amount, or (3) its assets are 10% or more of the total assets of all segments. Two or more internally reported business segments or geographical segments that are substantially similar may be combined as a single business or geographical segment. If total external revenue attributable to reportable segments constitutes less than 75% of total consolidated revenue, additional segments should be identified as reportable segments, even if they do not meet any of the foregoing 10% thresholds until at least 75% of total consolidated revenue is included in reportable segments.

The following information must be disclosed for each primary reportable segment:

- Revenue from external customers.
- Revenues from transactions with other segments.
- Segment result (i.e., profit or loss).
- The carrying amount of assets.
- The amount of liabilities.
- Total cost during the period of acquiring segment assets expected to be used over more than one period.
- Depreciation and amortization expense.
- The total amount of significant non-cash expenses (other than depreciation and amortization).

Segment profit or loss should be shown separately for continuing and discontinued operations (and prior period information should be restated based on the latest period's classifications).

If the primary reporting format is based on business segments, the following information should be disclosed for each reportable segment based on its secondary reporting format:

- Revenue from external customers (based on customer location for each geographical segment whose revenue from external sales represents 10% or more of the entity's total revenue from sales to all external customers).

- Segment assets by location for each geographical segment whose segment assets are 10% or more of the total assets of all geographical segments.
- The total cost during the period to acquire segment assets expected to be used over more than one period (by location of assets) for each geographical segment whose assets are 10% or more of all geographical segments.

If the primary reporting format is based on geographical segments, the following information should be disclosed for each business segment whose revenue from sales to external customers is 10% or more of consolidated sales or whose segment assets are 10% or more of the total of all assets of business segments:

- Revenue from external customers.
- The carrying amount of assets.
- Total cost during the period of acquiring segment assets expected to be used over more than one period.

If the primary reporting format is based on the geographical location of assets that differs from the location of customers, disclosure must also be made of revenue from external customers for each customer-based geographical segment whose revenue from external customers is 10% or more of consolidated revenue from sales to all external customers. If the primary reporting format is based on the geographical location of customers that differs from the location of assets, the following information should be disclosed for each asset-based geographical segment whose revenue from sales to external customers or segment assets are 10% or more of consolidated sales or assets:

- The total carrying amount of assets by location.
- Total cost during the period of acquiring segment assets expected to be used over more than one period (by location of assets).

If not provided elsewhere, disclosure should be made of (1) the types of products and services included in each reported business segment, and (2) the composition of each reported geographical segment.

## ¶ 3504. Under the Provisions of IFRS 8

An operating segment is a component of an entity:

- That engages in business activities from which it may earn revenues and incur expenses (including revenues and expenses relating to transactions with other components of the same entity).
- Whose operating results are regularly reviewed by the entity's chief operating decision maker to make decisions about resources to be allocated to the segment and assess its performance.
- For which discrete financial information is available.

The term "chief operating decision maker" identifies a function, not necessarily a manager with a specific title. That function is to allocate resources to and assess the performance of the operating segments of an entity. The chief operating decision maker (CODM) of an entity may be its chief executive officer or chief operating officer but it may be a group of executive directors or others.

A reportable segment (i.e., one for which information must be disclosed) is one that is an operating segment (or is the result of aggregating two or more operating segments) and that exceeds specific quantitative thresholds.

Two or more operating segments may be aggregated into a single operating segment if the segments have similar economic characteristics and they are similar in each of the following respects:

- The nature of the products and services.
- The nature of the production processes.
- The type or class of customer for their products and services.
- The methods used to distribute their products or provide their services.
- If applicable, the nature of the regulatory environment.

Separate reporting is required for an operating segment (including a segment resulting from aggregation) that meets any of the following quantitative thresholds:

- Its reported revenue, including both sales to external customers and inter-segment sales or transfers, is 10% or more of the combined revenue (internal and external) of all operating segments.
- The absolute amount of its reported profit or loss is 10% or more of the greater of (1) the combined reported profit of all operating segments that did not report a loss, and (2) the combined reported loss of all operating segments that reported a loss.
- Its assets are 10% or more of the combined assets of all operating segments

Operating segments that do not meet any of the quantitative thresholds may be considered reportable if management believes that information about the segment would be useful to users of the financial statements. If the total external revenue reported by operating segments constitutes less than 75% of the entity's revenue, additional operating segments must be identified as reportable segments (even if they do not meet the quantitative thresholds) until at least 75% of the entity's revenue is included in reportable segments. Information about non-reportable segments and other business activities should be combined in a category described as "all other."

The following information is required to be disclosed for each reportable segment:

- Factors used to identify reportable segments, including the basis of organization.
- Types of products and services from which each operating segment derives its revenues.
- A measure of profit or loss.
- Revenues from transactions with external customers.
- Revenues from transactions with other operating segments.

- Interest revenue.
- Interest expense.
- Depreciation and amortization.
- Unusual items.
- Equity in the profit or loss of associates and joint ventures accounted for by the equity method.
- Income tax expense or benefit.
- Significant non-cash items (other than depreciation and amortization).
- Total assets.

In addition to the foregoing data, reconciliations of the following to corresponding amounts on the entity's (consolidated) financial statements are required for the aggregate of all segments:

- Revenue.
- Profit or loss.
- Total assets.
- Every other significant item.

The following information is required to be disclosed on an entity-wide basis unless it is disclosed as part of the information about reportable segments:

- Revenues from external customers for each product and service or each group of similar products and services unless it is impracticable to do so.
- The following geographic amounts unless it is impracticable to do so:

  —Revenues from external customers (1) attributed to the entity's country of domicile, and (2) all foreign countries in total from which the segment derives significant revenues.

  —Non-current assets located (1) in the enterprise's country of domicile, and (2) in all foreign countries in total in which the segment holds significant assets.

Disclosure is also required of the fact of reliance on a single external customer from which 10% or more of revenues are derived; the amount of revenue earned from each such single customer must be reported and the applicable segment (or segments) must be identified.

# ¶ 3600. Share-Based Payment Arrangements

## U.S. GAAP

## ¶ 3601. Main Authoritative Sources

- SFAS No. 123(R), *Share-Based Payment*

## ¶ 3602. Share-Based Transactions in General

Generally, goods or services obtained in a share-based payment transaction are recognized at the time such goods or services are acquired or received, with a corresponding increase in equity or a liability, depending on whether the instruments granted satisfy the equity or liability classification criteria. As the goods or services are disposed of or consumed, the cost thereof is recognized against income.

If the fair value of goods or services received in a share-based payment transaction with non-employees is more reliably measurable than the fair value of the equity instruments issued, the fair value of the goods or services received should be used to measure the transaction. If, however, the fair value of the equity instruments issued is more reliably measurable than the fair value of the consideration received, the transaction should be measured based on the fair value of the equity instruments issued. A share-based payment transaction with employees should be measured based on the fair value (or in certain situations a so-called calculated value or intrinsic value) of the equity instruments issued.

## ¶ 3603. Equity Awards to Employees

Generally, the measurement objective for equity instruments is to estimate their fair value at the grant date for the equity instruments the entity is obligated to issue when employees have rendered requisite service and otherwise satisfied the conditions necessary to earn the right to benefit therefrom. The estimate of fair value should be based on the share price and other relevant factors, including restrictions and conditions inherent in the equity instruments awarded. The date of grant is the date on which the employer and affected employees reach a mutual understanding of the key terms and conditions of the award. Awards that are subject to shareholder approval are deemed granted when such approval is obtained; likewise, awards that must be approved by the board of directors and/or management are considered granted when such approval is received.

The fair value of equity share options (and similar instruments) should be measured based on observable market prices of options with the same or similar terms and conditions, if available. If observable market prices of identical or similar instruments are not available, fair value should be estimated by applying a valuation technique. Among such acceptable techniques are a lattice model (which includes a binomial model), a closed-form model (e.g., the Black-Scholes-Merton model), and a Monte Carlo simulation model. The model used must take into account the following factors:

- The exercise price of the option.

- The expected term of the option, including its contractual term and the effects of employees' expected exercise and post-vesting employment behavior.

- The current price of the underlying shares.

- Expected volatility of the price of the underlying shares over the expected term of the option.

- Expected dividends on the underlying shares for the term of the option.

- The risk-free rate over the term of the option.

If, for a nonpublic company, it is not practicable to estimate expected volatility of its share price, historical volatility of an appropriate industry sector index may be substituted for expected volatility of the entity's own shares in estimating fair value (referred to as a calculated value). In addition, in rare situations, because of the complexity of the instrument's terms, it may not be possible to estimate fair value, in which case, the intrinsic value method should be applied (and remeasured at each reporting date through the date of exercise or settlement). Under the intrinsic value method, the final measure of compensation cost is equal to the intrinsic value at settlement or exercise, with compensation cost for each period computed as the change in intrinsic value during that period. Note that, even if it subsequently becomes possible to estimate fair value, continued use of the intrinsic value method is required for such instruments.

Compensation cost for employee share-based awards classified as equity should be recognized over the requisite service period. For a graded vesting award having only service conditions, compensation cost may be recognized either on a straight-line basis over the requisite service period for (1) each separately vesting portion of the award (referred to as the graded vesting attribution method), or (2) the entire award. If an award requires satisfaction of one or more market, performance, or service conditions, compensation cost should be recognized as long as the requisite service has been rendered (but should not be recognized if the requisite service has not been rendered). Performance and service conditions that affect vesting should not be reflected in the estimation of the award's fair value at the date of grant because those conditions represent restrictions stemming from the forfeitability of instruments to which employees have not yet earned rights. The effect of a market condition, however, should be considered in estimating fair value at the grant date because such a condition is not deemed to be a vesting condition (i.e., an award is not forfeited solely because a market condition is not satisfied).

Options issued as compensation to employees should be classified as liabilities (1) if the cash settlement feature can be exercised only upon the occurrence of a contingent event that is outside the employee's control (e.g., an initial public offering), and (2) such event is deemed probable to occur. Options initially classified as equity that subsequently become liabilities (because the contingent cash settlement event is probable of occurring) should be accounted for in a manner similar to that of a modification of an award that changes the award's character from equity to a liability. An award indexed to a factor in addition to the entity's share price that is not a market, performance, or service condition (e.g., indexed to the market price for a commodity) should be classified as a liability and the additional factor should be taken into account in estimating the award's fair value.

Changes in fair value (or in intrinsic value for nonpublic entities) of a share-based payment liability should be recognized as compensation cost over the requisite service period (based on the percentage of requisite service rendered each period). Changes in fair (or intrinsic) value of a liability that occurs after the requisite service period should be recognized as compensation cost of the period in which the changes occur. Any difference between the amount for which a liability award is settled and its fair value on the settlement date represents an adjustment of compensation cost in the settlement period.

Liability awards should be measured in the same manner as equity awards (i.e., at fair value). For liability awards, however, the measurement date is the settlement date (rather than the date of grant). Public entities must remeasure fair value at each reporting date through the settlement date, and compensation cost for such entities should be based on the change in fair value for each reporting period. Nonpublic entities may choose to measure share-based payment liabilities at fair value or intrinsic value (and, as is the case with awards classified as equity, a nonpublic entity may use calculated value as a substitute for fair value).

A modification of the terms or conditions of an equity award should be treated as an exchange of the original award for a new award. The effects of a modification should be measured as follows:

- The incremental (additional) compensation cost should be computed as any excess of the fair value of the modified award over the fair value of the original award immediately before modification. The effect of the modification on the number of instruments expected to vest also should be reflected in determining incremental compensation cost. The estimate at the modification date of the portion of the award expected to vest should be subsequently adjusted, if necessary.

- Total recognized compensation cost for an equity award must be at least equal to the fair value of the award at the grant date, unless at the date of the modification, the performance or service conditions of the original award are not expected to be satisfied. Thus, total compensation cost at the modification date should comprise (1) the portion of fair value of the original award at its date of grant for which requisite service is expected to be (or already has been) rendered, and (2) the incremental cost attributable to the modification (subsequently adjusted, as necessary, for changes in the estimated number of instruments for which requisite service is expected to be rendered and the probable outcome of performance conditions).

- Incremental compensation cost for awards measured at intrinsic value should be computed as the difference (if any) between intrinsic value of the modified award and any intrinsic value of the original award immediately before modification.

## ¶ 3604. Employee Share Purchase Plans

An employee share purchase plan meeting all of the following criteria does not give rise to recognizable compensation cost:

- The terms of the plan are no less favorable than those available to all holders of the same class of shares or a purchase discount from the market price is not more than the per share amount of share issuance costs that would have been incurred to raise a significant amount of capital through a public offering; note that a discount of greater than 5% of the market price that cannot be justified under this condition results in compensation cost equal to the entire amount of the discount.

- Substantially all employees meeting limited employment qualifications are allowed to participate on an equitable basis.

- The plan has no option features other than that (1) employees are permitted no more than 31 days after the purchase price of the shares has been set to enroll in the plan, (2) the purchase price is based solely on the market price at the date of purchase, and (3) employees are permitted to cancel participation before the purchase date and obtain a refund of amounts previously paid in.

If an employee share purchase plan does not meet all of the foregoing conditions (and thus is deemed a compensatory plan), the requisite service period should be considered the period over which employees participate in the plan and pay for the shares.

IFRS

## ¶ 3605. Main Authoritative Sources

- IFRS 2, *Share-based Payment*

## ¶ 3606. Share-Based Transactions in General

Goods or services obtained or acquired in a share-based payment transaction should be recognized when the goods are received or as the services are received, with a corresponding increase in equity if the goods or services were received in an equity-settled share-based payment transaction or a corresponding increase in a liability if the goods or services were acquired in a cash-settled share-based payment transaction. When the goods or services received or acquired in a share-based payment transaction do not qualify for recognition as assets, they should be charged to profit or loss.

For equity-settled share-based payment transactions, the goods or services obtained should be measured at fair value of the goods or services received, unless that fair value cannot be estimated reliably, in which case they should be measured by reference to the fair value of the equity instruments granted.

## ¶ 3607. Equity Awards to Employees

For transactions with employees (and others providing similar services), fair value, which should be determined at the date of grant, is equal to estimated fair value of the equity instruments granted, because typically it is not possible to estimate reliably the fair value of the services received. The grant date is the date at which the entity and employees agree to a share-based payment arrangement; if that agreement is subject to an approval process (e.g., by shareholders), the grant date is the date on which such approval is obtained.

Fair value should be determined, based on market prices if available, taking into account the terms and conditions upon which those equity instruments were granted. If market prices are not available, fair value should be estimated using a valuation technique (i.e., an option pricing model) to estimate what the price of those equity instruments would have been on the measurement (i.e., grant) date in an arm's-length transaction between knowledgeable, willing parties. The valuation technique must be consistent with generally accepted valuation methodologies for pricing financial instruments and must incorporate all factors and assumptions that knowledgeable, willing market participants would consider in setting the price. Option pricing models should take into account, as a minimum, the following factors:

- The exercise price of the option.
- The life of the option.
- The current price of the underlying shares.
- The expected volatility of the share price.
- Dividends expected on the shares (if appropriate).
- The risk-free interest rate for the life of the option.

In rare cases, when the fair value of the equity instruments granted at the measurement date cannot be reliably estimated, the equity instruments should be measured at their intrinsic value (i.e., the difference between fair value of the underlying shares and the award's exercise price); and subsequent change in intrinsic value at each reporting date should be recognized in profit or loss.

If the equity instruments granted do not vest until the counterparty completes a specified period of service, consideration for services received (i.e., compensation cost) should be recognized over the vesting period. If vesting depends on service and the achievement of a performance condition, the vesting period should be estimated at the grant date, based on the most likely outcome of the performance condition (with subsequent revisions made based on changes in the estimated vesting period). At the vesting date, the cumulative amount of compensation cost recognized should be based on the number of equity instruments actually vested (i.e., on a cumulative basis; no amount is recognized for equity instruments that did not vest because of failure to satisfy the vesting conditions).

For cash-settled share-based payment transactions, a liability should be established at fair value (based on application of an option pricing model), with subsequent changes in fair value recognized in profit or loss and taking into account the terms and conditions on which the share appreciation rights were granted and the extent to which the employees have rendered service to date. For share-based payment transactions in which the terms of the arrangement provide either the entity or the counterparty with the choice of whether the entity settles the transaction in cash (or other assets) or by issuing equity instruments, such transactions should be accounted for (1) as a cash-settled share-based payment transaction if a liability has been incurred, or (2) as an equity-settled share-based payment transaction if no liability has been incurred.

Upon modification to the terms and conditions of an equity award, the minimum amount of compensation cost recognized should be the fair value of the original award (i.e., as if it had not been modified). In addition, for modifications that increase fair value, the incremental fair value of any modifications must be recognized (i.e., the difference between the fair value of the modified and original awards, both measured as of the modification date).

## ¶ 3608. Employee Share Purchase Plans

IFRS does not address the topic of employee share purchase plans.

# ¶ 3700. Subsequent Events

## U.S. GAAP

## ¶ 3701. Main Authoritative Sources

- SAS No. 1, *Codification of Auditing Standards and Procedures* (AU 560, "Subsequent Events")
- SFAS No. 5, *Accounting for Contingencies*

A subsequent event is an event (or transaction) that occurs after the date of the financial statements but prior to their issuance. There are two types of subsequent events: (1) those that provide additional evidence in respect of conditions that existed at the balance-sheet date, and (2) those that provide evidence in respect of conditions that did not exist at the balance-sheet date but arose after that date.

Type I subsequent events consist of those events that provide additional evidence with respect to conditions that existed at the date of the financial statements and affect the estimates inherent in the process of preparing financial statements. All information that becomes available after the date of the financial statements but prior to their issuance should be considered in the evaluation of the conditions on which the estimates were based, and the financial statements should be adjusted for any changes resulting from the new evidence.

Type II subsequent events consist of those events that provide evidence with respect to conditions that did not exist at the date of the financial statements. Instead, the event or transaction arose after the balance-sheet date but before the financial statements were issued. Financial statements should not be adjusted for the effects of Type II events. Such events, if significant and necessary in order to keep the financial statements from being misleading, should be disclosed.

## IFRS

## ¶ 3702. Main Authoritative Sources

- IAS 10, *Events after the Balance Sheet Date*

Events after the balance sheet date (i.e., subsequent events) are events that occur between the balance sheet date and the date the financial statements are authorized for issuance. The two types of events after the balance sheet date are:

- Those that provide evidence of conditions that existed at the balance sheet date (referred to as adjusting events)
- Those that are indicative of conditions that arose after the balance sheet date (referred to as non-adjusting events).

Financial statements should be adjusted for events after the balance sheet date providing evidence of conditions existing at that date; although the financial statements should not be adjusted for events indicating conditions arising after the balance sheet date, disclosure of the nature and estimated effect of such events should be made if they are deemed sufficiently material such that non-disclosure could influence decisions of financial statement users.

The financial statements should not be prepared on the basis of a going concern if, after the balance sheet date, management determines either that it intends to liquidate the entity or to cease operations (or that it has no realistic alternative but to do so).

# ¶ 3800. Major Proposals Outstanding

## ¶ 3801. Major Proposals Outstanding

Following are summary discussions of major FASB, IASB, and IFRIC proposals outstanding at press time. Note that exposure drafts are subject to redeliberations following their comment periods; thus, upon adoption, final rules may differ (sometimes substantially) from proposed rules. Moreover, upon redeliberation, (1) action on a proposal may be significantly (or indefinitely) delayed, (2) the topic may be removed from the standard setter's agenda, or (3) the exposure draft may be eliminated as a self-standing document because its topic has been incorporated into a broader project.

U.S. GAAP

## ¶ 3802. Earnings per Share (proposed SFAS)

The proposed standard would amend SFAS No. 128, *Earnings per Share*, as follows:

- Currently, in computing year-to-date diluted EPS under the treasury stock method, the number of incremental shares to be added to the denominator is determined using a year-to-date weighted average of the number of such incremental shares in each quarterly diluted EPS calculation. As proposed, the number of incremental shares in year-to-date diluted EPS would be computed using the average market price of the common shares for the year-to-date period.

- In applying the treasury stock method to a share-based instrument classified as a liability but potentially settled in shares, the carrying amount of the extinguished liability (upon issuance of the shares) would be treated as assumed proceeds in the computation of incremental shares.

- Presently, in the computation of basic EPS, contingently issuable shares must be considered as outstanding as of the date that all necessary conditions for their issuance have been met. As proposed, that requirement would include common shares to be issued upon conversion of a mandatorily convertible security (instrument) from the date the conversion becomes mandatory, even if to do so would result in anti-dilution. In addition, a mandatorily convertible instrument would be defined as one requiring the holder to exchange the instrument (with little or no additional consideration) for a fixed number of common shares at a specified or determinable date or upon an event certain to occur.

- Currently, there is a presumption that contracts that may be settled in stock or in cash will be settled in stock, unless past experience or a stated policy provides a reasonable basis that they will be settled in cash (the rebuttable presumption). As proposed, such contracts would be assumed to be settled in stock (i.e., the rebuttable presumption would be removed). The rebuttable presumption would also be removed and would require share settlement to be assumed (but only if dilutive) for any instrument that permits or requires share settlement under any circumstances (unless the only circumstance permitting or requiring share settlement is in the event of the issuer's legal bankruptcy).

## ¶ 3803. Financial Guarantee Insurance Contracts (proposed SFAS)

The proposed SFAS would clarify how SFAS No. 60, *Accounting and Reporting by Insurance Enterprises*, applies to financial guarantee insurance contracts and provide guidance on the method of accounting for such contracts.

To be within the scope of the proposed standard, a financial guarantee insurance contract must obligate the insurance entity to pay a claim upon the occurrence of a default in the amount for which the claim is submitted. A liability would be recognized for unearned premium revenue at inception of the contract in an amount equal to the present value of the premium due over the guarantee's contractual (rather than expected) term. The discount rate to be applied in determining the receivable for future premiums (if any) would have to reflect the policyholder's credit standing at inception, with the discount accreted over the contract period. Subsequently, the premium receivable would have to be evaluated for collectibility, with any corresponding adjustments made to bad-debt expense.

Premium revenue would be recognized over the period of the contract based on the ratio of (1) contractual payments under the financial obligation made during the period by the issuer of the financial obligation to (2) the total of all insured contractual payments to be made by the issuer over the contract period. Upon refunding (i.e., retirement of the original financial obligation before maturity and replacement thereof with a new obligation), the entire amount of nonrefundable premium revenue related to the retired contract would be recognized (together with any associated deferred acquisition costs). Unearned premium revenue (a liability) would be recognized on the new contract at the amount that the insurance enterprise would charge to insure a similar financial obligation in a separate (i.e., standalone) transaction; any difference between the amount of that premium and the amount of the actual premium would be recognized in current earnings.

A claim liability would be recognized when the amount of the claim loss will, based on expected cash flows, exceed the amount of unearned premium revenue. When a claim liability is recognized, any associated previously deferred acquisition costs would also be recognized. The claim liability would be initially measured as the present value of probability-weighted expected cash outflows using a risk-adjusted discount rate (i.e., the risk-free rate increased by a factor for the insurer's credit standing). Subsequently, revised expected cash flows would be discounted (applying the same rate used at inception), with any adjustments to the claim liability recognized as claim expense (as a change in accounting estimate).

## ¶ 3804. Disclosure Requirements for Derivatives and Hedging (proposed SFAS)

The proposed standard would revise and enhance the disclosure requirements in SFAS No. 133, *Accounting for Derivative Instruments and Hedging Activities*, for derivatives used as hedging instruments and related hedged items, as follows:

- A discussion would be required of the entity's objectives for holding or issuing derivative instruments distinguishing between derivatives used for risk management purposes (based on the instrument's primary risk exposure) and those used for all other purposes.

- The following information would be required in tabular format in respect of derivatives held or issued that qualify as hedging instruments (by primary underlying risk, accounting designation, and purpose):

  —Notional amounts for derivatives held at the end of the period.

  —The location and fair value of derivatives reported in the balance sheet (separately for asset and liability values within each purpose category).

  —The location and amount of gains and losses reported in the income statement for derivatives and related hedged items held at the end of the period. Such gains and losses would have to be presented separately for (1) derivatives in fair value hedges, (2) hedged items in fair value hedges, (3) the ineffective portion and the amounts excluded from effectiveness testing for derivatives used in cash flow and net investment hedges, (4) the effective portion for cash flow and net investment hedges recognized in other comprehensive income, (5) the effective portion for cash flow and net investment hedges originally reported in other comprehensive income that has been reclassified into current earnings, and (6) derivatives not designated and qualifying as hedging instruments.

  —The location and amount of gains and losses on derivatives and related hedged items that (1) are no longer held at the end of the period, or (2) are no longer in a designated hedging relationship at the end of the period.

  —The estimated magnitude that leverage factors have on the notional amount and underlying risk of a derivative instrument. Note that individual tables would be required, as applicable, by interest rate risk, credit risk, foreign exchange risk, and overall price risk. The accounting designation categories within each such table would have to include, when applicable, derivatives (1) used for fair value hedges, (2) used for cash flow hedges, (3) used for net investment hedges, and (4) not used as hedging instruments.

- Disclosure would be required of (1) the existence and nature of contingent features within derivatives that are used as hedging instruments and the circumstances under which such features could be triggered, (2) the aggregate fair value of derivatives containing contingent features, and (3) the aggregate fair value of assets that would be required to be posted as collateral (or actually transferred) if contingent features are triggered.

- Disclosure would be required of (1) the maximum loss that could be incurred as a result of counterparty credit risk based on the gross fair value of derivatives in asset positions (and assuming that any collateral held proved to be of no value), (2) the aggregate fair value of derivatives in asset positions, net of collateral posted by counterparties, (3) the entity's policy for entering into netting arrangements to mitigate credit risk of derivatives, information about such arrangements, and a brief description of the terms thereof (including the amount by which the arrangements would reduce the maximum loss due to credit risk), and (4) the entity's policy of requiring collateral or other security to support derivative instruments subject to credit risk, information about the entity's access to such collateral, and the nature, amount, and a brief description of collateral or other security supporting derivative instruments.

## ¶ 3805. Hierarchy of GAAP (proposed SFAS)

The proposed standard would modify the hierarchy of GAAP sources and move it to the GAAP literature, itself; as it now stands, the GAAP hierarchy is contained in SAS No. 69, *The Meaning of Present Fairly in Conformity with Generally Accepted Accounting Principles.* Although, for the most part, the Board would carry forward the existing hierarchy set forth in SAS No. 69, the proposed SFAS would make certain modifications, principally as follows:

- Categories of sources would be based on document type, rather than by their characteristics.

- Category (a) sources would be expanded to include FASB Staff Positions and FASB Statement 133 Implementation Issues, neither of which is addressed in SAS No. 69.

The new hierarchy would be categorized as follows:

Category (a). AICPA Accounting Research Bulletins and Accounting Principles Board Opinions not superseded by the FASB, FASB Statements of Financial Accounting Standards, FASB Interpretations, FASB Statement 133 Implementation Issues, and FASB Staff Positions. In addition, though not officially included within any category, rules, interpretive releases and staff accounting bulletins of the SEC would be considered category (a) sources for public companies.

Category (b). FASB Technical Bulletins, and, if cleared by the Board, AICPA Industry Audit and Accounting Guides and AICPA Statements of Position.

Category (c). AcSEC Practice Bulletins that have been cleared by the FASB and consensus positions of the FASB Emerging Issues Task Force.

Category (d). Implementation Guides (Qs and As) of the FASB Staff, AICPA Accounting Interpretations, and practices that are widely recognized either generally or in the industry.

If the accounting treatment for a transaction or event is not specified in a category (a) source, consideration would have to be given to whether such treatment is specified in a source from a lower category (and the treatment contained in such a source from the highest of the remaining categories (b)–(d) would have to be followed). If the accounting treatment is not specified in any of the categories, consideration would have to be given to (1) principles applied to similar transactions or events, unless such principles either explicitly prohibit application to the transaction or event in question, or prohibit application to other transactions or events by analogy, and (2) so-called other accounting literature. Sources of other accounting literature would include:

- FASB Concepts Statements (which would normally be deemed to be more influential than any other source in the category).

- AICPA Issues Papers.

- International Financial Reporting Standards.

- Pronouncements of other professional associations or regulatory agencies.

- Inquiries and Replies contained in AICPA Technical Practice Aids.

- Textbooks, handbooks, and articles.

An entity would be precluded from representing that its financial statements are presented in accordance with GAAP if the principles used departed from the GAAP hierarchy and such departure had a material effect on the financial statements.

## ¶ 3806. Share-Based Transactions and Participating Securities (proposed FSP)

It would be the Staff's position that rights to dividends (or dividend equivalents) providing a non-contingent transfer of value to the holder of share-based payment awards (even if the award remains unvested) constitute participation rights that should be included in the computation of earnings per share under the two-class method. Hence, a share-based award entitling holders to a non-forfeitable right to receive cash when dividends are paid on common stock would be deemed a participating security because the transfer of value is not contingent on the employee-holders performing additional services after the dividend declaration date. If, however, the cash dividends are forfeited if the award does not vest, the award would not be a participating security (because the transfer of value is contingent on vesting).

It would also be the Staff's position that a share-based award participating in undistributed earnings by way of a reduction in the exercise price would not be considered a participating security because the transfer of value to the holders is contingent upon the award being exercised.

In accordance with SFAS No. 123(R), *Share-Based Payment*, non-refundable dividends (or dividend equivalents) paid on awards that do not vest should be accounted for as additional compensation, whereas dividends paid on awards that do vest should be charged against retained earnings. It would thus be the Staff's position that dividends paid on awards that do not vest (or are not expected to vest) should not be included in the earnings allocation in computing earnings per share, because to do so would amount to double counting (i.e., the dividend would reduce earnings otherwise available to common stockholders in the forms of additional compensation cost and distributed earnings).

## ¶ 3807. Transfers of Financial Assets and Repurchase Transactions (proposed FSP)

SFAS No. 140, *Accounting for Transfers and Servicing of Financial Assets and Extinguishments of Liabilities*, requires all involvements of a transferor with a transferred financial asset to be considered in determining whether the transferor has surrendered control (i.e., one of the conditions for applying sale accounting)—even if those involvements take place subsequent to the transfer itself. Among other criteria in SFAS No. 140, to have surrendered control, the transferor and transferee must not have entered into an agreement obligating the transferor to repurchase the transferred asset prior to its maturity. The proposed FSP addresses the specific issue of whether there may be circumstances that would permit a transferor and transferee to evaluate the accounting for a transferred asset separately from that of a repurchase agreement (i.e., a repurchase financing), rather than presumptively as a linked transaction.

It would be the Staff's position that a transferor and transferee would have to account for a transfer of a financial asset separately from a related repurchase financing (whether it was entered into simultaneously or subsequently) if (1) the transactions have a valid and distinct business or economic purpose requiring them to be entered into separately, and (2) the repurchase financing does not result in the transferor regaining control over the financial asset. To qualify for separate accounting treatment, all of the following conditions would have to be satisfied:

- The initial transfer and the repurchase financing could not be contractually contingent on each other.
- The repurchase financing would have to provide the initial transferor with full recourse to the transferee upon default.
- The transferee's agreement to repurchase the previously transferred financial asset would have to be at a fixed price (and could not be set at fair value).
- The transferred financial asset must carry a quoted price in an active market and the initial transfer of the financial asset and the repurchase financing would have to be executed at market rates.
- The initial transferee/borrower would have to maintain rights to the collateral.
- The initial transferor/lender could not sell or re-pledge the collateral at any time prior to the settlement of the repurchase financing, unless the asset is readily obtainable.
- The maturity date of the repurchase financing would have to be earlier than that of the financial asset (i.e., the financial asset and the repurchase agreement could not carry coterminous maturity dates).

If the transactions do not meet all of the foregoing criteria, the initial transfer and repurchase financing would be deemed a linked transaction that would have to be further evaluated to determine whether it meets the conditions for sale accounting. If such conditions are not met, the linked transaction would be accounted for based on the economic substance of the combined transactions (which, generally, represent a forward contract to be accounted for in accordance with SFAS No. 133, *Accounting for Derivative Instruments and Hedging Activities*).

## ¶ 3808. Convertible Debt Settled in Cash upon Conversion (proposed FSP)

APB Opinion No. 14, *Accounting for Convertible Debt and Debt Issues with Stock Purchase Warrants*, does not apply to convertible debt instruments that may be settled in cash upon their conversion. The proposed FSP addresses such instruments and would require separate accounting for the liability and equity components; in addition, it would require that the discount attributable to the liability component be amortized over the expected life of a similar liability that does not have an associated equity element.

Upon issuance, the carrying amount of the liability component to be recognized would be equal to the fair value of a similar liability. The equity element to be recognized would be calculated as the difference between (1) the initial proceeds from the combined instrument, and (2) the amount ascribed to the liability component.

Any excess of the principal amount of the liability component over its initial fair value (i.e., a discount) would be amortized using the interest method over the expected life of a similar liability not having an associated equity component. The equity component (i.e., the conversion option) would not be subsequently remeasured as long as it continues to meet the conditions for equity classification. If reclassification of the conversion option to that of a liability is required, the difference between the amount previously recognized (in equity) and the conversion option's fair value at the reclassification date would be accounted for as an adjustment to stockholders' equity. Once reclassified to a liability, any gains or losses attributable to changes in fair value would be charged or credited to results of operations.

If a modification made to a covered convertible debt instrument does not qualify as an extinguishment, a new effective rate for the liability component would have to be determined. If an instrument is modified or exchanged in a manner qualifying it for extinguishment and the new convertible debt instrument will not be settled for cash upon conversion, the new instrument would be accounted for under APB Opinion No. 14 (i.e., with no separate accounting for its liability and equity components).

Upon settlement through the issuance of cash, stock (or any combination thereof) or modification or exchange of the instrument resulting in an extinguishment, the fair value of the consideration given would be allocated to the liability component, with the remainder allocated to the conversion option (i.e., the equity component). Any difference between the assigned fair value of the liability immediately before derecognition and the liability's carrying amount at that date would be recognized as a gain or loss on extinguishment. The conversion option would be accounted for as a reacquisition, with any difference between the amount of consideration given that was ascribed to the equity component and its carrying amount recognized as an adjustment to stockholders' equity. If additional consideration was given to induce early conversion, upon derecognition, a loss would be recorded in an amount equal to the excess fair value of all such additional consideration transferred over the fair value of consideration issuable under the original conversion terms.

## ¶ 3809. Determining the Useful Lives of Intangible Assets (proposed FSP)

SFAS No. 142, *Goodwill and Other Intangible Assets*, as it now stands, requires that in determining the useful life of a recognized intangible asset consideration should be given, among other entity-specific factors, to legal, regulatory, or contractual provisions that enable renewal or extension of the asset's life without substantial cost, provided (1) there is evidence to support renewal, and (2) it can be accomplished without material modifications of existing terms and conditions.

As a practical matter, when an agreement contains renewal or extension terms, the useful life of an intangible asset is typically shorter than the period of expected cash flows, which is the approach used to measure the fair value of an asset acquired in a business combination. Such difference may relate to the level of negotiations involved in renewing or extending the implicit terms of the underlying arrangement (i.e., terms that are not explicitly included in the agreement).

Accordingly, the proposed FSP would amend the factors in SFAS No. 142 to be considered in developing renewal or extension terms used when determining an intangible asset's useful life to allow consideration of an entity's own assumptions about renewal or extension of an arrangement. Specifically:

- The factor currently included in SFAS No. 142 for determining an intangible asset's useful life requiring consideration of legal, regulatory, or contractual provisions that enable renewal or extension of the asset's life without substantial cost, provided (1) there is evidence to support renewal, and (2) it can be accomplished without material modifications of existing terms and conditions would be removed.

- A factor would be added permitting an entity to take account of its own historical experience in respect of the renewal or extension of similar arrangements (but consistent with the asset's intended use by the entity), even if those arrangements do not contain explicit renewal or extension provisions; in the absence of such experience, consideration would have to be given to the assumptions that market participants would make about renewal or extension (consistent with their highest and best use of the asset).

## ¶ 3810. Measuring the Fair Value of a Liability (proposed FSP)

SFAS No. 157, *Fair Value Measurements*, defines the fair value of a liability as the price that would be paid to transfer the liability in an orderly transaction between market participants at the measurement date. Pursuant to that definition, the liability to the counterparty is presumed to continue (i.e., it is not settled). Also, in accordance with SFAS No. 157, the fair value of a liability must reflect the reporting entity's own credit risk, which remains at the same level before and after transfer of the liability. In many situations, however, an entity would extinguish the liability by settling the obligation directly with the counterparty, rather than by paying another entity to assume it, and, if the liability were to be transferred, the transferee may not have the same credit (i.e., non-performance) risk as that of the transferor. In addition, in some cases, there is a lack of observable markets or observable inputs for the transfer of a liability (particularly when the liability continues to exist but the original obligor is completely relieved of any obligation to the counterparty). Hence, because of such factors, the measurement of the fair value of a liability could embody a hypothetical attribute (i.e., it would be based on the notion of a transfer that would not actually occur in the marketplace). Accordingly, the proposed FSP would amend SFAS No. 157 to clarify the process by which the fair value of a liability should be determined.

The proposed FSP would amend SFAS No. 157 as follows:

- It would clarify that a quoted price for the identical obligation in an active market (i.e., a Level 1 input) represents the best evidence of the fair value of a liability and that such price should be used as the fair value measurement for both the obligor and the asset holder (i.e., the market participant to whom the liability would be hypothetically transferred).

- It would require that, in the absence of a quoted market price in an active market, the reporting entity (i.e., the obligor) should measure fair value of the liability at the amount it would receive as proceeds if it were to issue that liability (to a market participant) at the measurement date, which would yield an equivalent of the amount that market participants would demand to assume the reporting entity's liability (i.e., fair value).

IFRS

# ¶ 3811. Related Parties (proposed IFRS)

The proposed IFRS would amend IAS 24, *Related Party Disclosure*, as follows:

- Exempt state-controlled entities from certain disclosure requirements if (1) the entity is a related party only because the reporting entity is controlled or significantly influenced by a state (i.e., a national, regional, or local government) and the other entity is controlled or significantly influenced by that state, and (2) there are no indicators that the reporting entity influenced or was influenced by that entity.

- Revise the definition of a related party to the reporting entity to include a *person* or a close member of the family of that person who (1) is a member of the key management personnel of the reporting entity or a parent of the reporting entity, (2) has control over the reporting entity, or (3) has joint control or significant influence over the reporting entity.

- Revise the definition of a related party to the reporting entity to include an *entity* if:

  —The entity and the reporting entity are members of the same group (i.e., each parent, subsidiary, and fellow subsidiary is related to the others).

  —The reporting entity is an associate or joint venture of the entity (or of a member of a group of which the entity is a member).

—The entity is an associate or joint venture of the reporting entity (or of a member of a group of which the reporting entity is a member).

—The entity is a post-employment benefit plan for the benefit of employees of either the reporting entity or an entity related to the reporting entity.

—A member of the key management personnel of the entity or a parent of the entity has control, joint control, or significant influence over or significant voting power in the reporting entity.

• Revise the definition of a related party transaction to clarify that such a transaction is one between the reporting entity and a related party.

## ¶ 3812. Provisions and Contingencies (proposed IFRS)

The proposed standard would amend IAS 37, *Provisions, Contingent Liabilities and Contingent Assets.* Following is a brief discussion of the principal proposed revisions.

• IAS 37 defines a provision as a liability of uncertain timing or amount; the term "non-financial liability" would replace the term "provision."

• The terms "contingent liability" and "contingent asset" would be replaced by the umbrella term "contingency" to refer to uncertainty about (1) the amount that will be required to settle a liability, rather than uncertainty about whether a liability exists, and (2) the amount of the future economic benefits embodied in an asset, rather than uncertainty about whether an asset exists.

• A liability for which the settlement amount is contingent on one or more uncertain future events would be recognized independently of the probability that the uncertain future event (or events) will occur or fail to occur.

• Contingent assets, which are not currently permitted to be recognized, but that otherwise meet the definition of an asset, would fall under the scope of IAS 38, *Intangible Assets.*

• The definition of a constructive obligation would be amended to clarify that the actions of an entity must result in other parties having a valid expectation that they can reasonably rely on the entity to discharge its responsibilities.

• If an entity has a non-financial liability arising from an unconditional obligation that is accompanied by a conditional obligation, the probability recognition criterion would be applied to the unconditional obligation rather than the conditional obligation.

• A non-financial liability would be measured at the amount that an entity would rationally pay to settle the present obligation or to transfer it to a third party on the balance sheet date; note that an expected cash flow approach could be used as the basis for measuring a non-financial liability.

• If an entity has an unconditional right to receive reimbursement, that right would be recognized as an asset if it can be measured reliably.

• IAS 37 defines an onerous contract as one in which the unavoidable costs of meeting its obligations exceed the economic benefits expected; as proposed, if a contract will become onerous as a result of an entity's own action, the liability would not be recognized until the entity has taken that action.

- In respect of a restructuring, a non-financial liability for a cost associated with a restructuring would be recognized only when the definition of a liability has been satisfied for such cost; thus, a cost associated with a restructuring would be recognized as a liability on the same basis as if that cost arose independently of the restructuring.

## ¶ 3813. Exposures Qualifying for Hedge Accounting (proposed IFRS)

The proposed standard would amend IAS 39, *Financial Instruments: Recognition and Measurement*, to clarify the circumstances under which exposure to a financial instrument may be designated as a hedged item. Generally a financial instrument could be designated as a hedged item for one or more of the following risks:

- Interest rate risk (i.e., the risk that the fair value or future cash flows of the financial instrument will fluctuate because of changes in market interest rates).

- Foreign currency risk (i.e., the risk that the fair value or future cash flows of the financial instrument will fluctuate because of changes in foreign exchange rates).

- Credit risk.

- Prepayment risk.

- The risks associated with the contractually specified cash flows of a recognized financial instrument (e.g., the cash flows of a financial asset that fluctuates with the rate of inflation because, of itself, inflation qualifies as a contractually specified cash flow).

In addition, the following portions of the cash flows of a financial instrument could be designated as a hedged item:

- The cash flows of a financial instrument for part of its time period to maturity (referred to as a partial term hedge).

- A percentage of the cash flows of a financial instrument.

- The cash flows of a financial instrument associated with a one-sided risk of that instrument (e.g., the cash flows resulting from a foreign exchange rate falling below a specified level).

- Any contractually specified cash flows of a financial instrument that are independent of the other cash flows of that instrument (e.g., the first four interest payments on a floating rate financial liability).

- The portion of the cash flows of an interest-bearing financial instrument that is equivalent to a financial instrument with a risk-free rate.

- The portion of the cash flows of an interest-bearing financial instrument that is equivalent to a financial instrument with a quoted fixed or variable interbank rate.

## ¶ 3814. IFRS for Small and Medium-Sized Entities (proposed IFRS)

The proposed IFRS is intended to provide a simplified, self-contained set of accounting and financial reporting principles that are appropriate for smaller, non-listed companies (i.e., entities not having public accountability) but which are based on concepts included in the full set of IFRS that were developed primarily for listed companies. Essentially, the proposed IFRS reflects three major differences from the full set of IFRS: (1) topics deemed irrelevant to small and medium-sized entities (SMEs) have been omitted; (2) only the simplest option among choices in the complete set of IFRS has been included; and (3) various recognition and measurement principles have been simplified.

An entity would be considered to have public accountability if (1) it has issued debt or equity securities in a public market, or (2) it holds assets in a fiduciary capacity for a broad range of parties (e.g., banks, insurance companies, broker-dealers, pension funds, mutual funds, investment banks). Note that adoption of the IFRS for SMEs would be a matter for each country to decide.

Certain topics contained in the full set of IFRS have been completely omitted from the proposed IFRS for SMEs on the assumption that such topics are largely irrelevant to small and medium-sized entities. In cases for which an omitted topic is relevant to an SME, the proposed IFRS would contain a cross reference to the applicable standard. The omitted topics include:

- Price-level reporting in a hyperinflationary environment.
- Equity-settled share-based payment arrangements.
- The fair-value determination for agricultural assets.
- Accounting for the exploration and evaluation of mineral resources.
- Interim reporting.
- Accounting for finance leases by lessors.
- Earnings per share.
- Segmental reporting.

Note that while SMEs would have to test goodwill for impairment in the same manner as their larger counterparts using the full set of IFRS, SMEs would be required to make such impairment tests much less frequently.

For situations in which a full IFRS provides an accounting policy choice, only the simpler option has been included in the proposed IFRS for SMEs. Note, though, that, on a country-by-country basis, SMEs might be allowed to use the other (i.e., the more complicated) option, which would be cross-referenced to the relevant full IFRS. The simpler options included in the proposed IFRS are:

- The cost-depreciation (rather than the fair value) model for investment property.

- The cost-amortization model (which includes impairment testing) rather than the revaluation model for property, plant, and equipment and intangible assets.

- All interest expense charged to current earnings (rather than capitalization of interest under certain conditions).

- The indirect (rather than the direct) method of reporting cash flows from operations in the cash flow statement.

- Use of any of the alternative methods of accounting for government grants and assistance.

Note that, in adopting the IFRS for SMEs, individual countries would be able to decide whether to permit SMEs to apply the more complicated options included in the full set of IFRS.

Recognition and measurement would be simplified for the following topics:

- Hedges.
- Held-to-maturity securities.
- Derecognition of a financial asset.
- Goodwill impairment testing.
- Research and development.
- Joint ventures.
- Defined-benefit plans.
- Share-based payment arrangements.
- Finance leases.
- First-time adoption of IFRS.

As proposed, the so-called fallback method would not be required (i.e., when an event or transaction is not addressed in the IFRS for SMEs, entities would not have to revert to the requirements of the full set of IFRS). In the absence of such guidance, SMEs would determine the appropriate accounting treatment (1) by analogy to similar and related specific guidance contained in the IFRS for SMEs, and (2) by reference to the definitions, recognition criteria, measurement concepts, and overarching principles included (but set out separately) within the IFRS for SMEs.

The IASB intends to update the IFRS for SMEs approximately once every two years.

## ¶ 3815. Determining the Cost of an Investment in Separate Financial Statements (proposed IFRS)

The proposed standard would amend IFRS 1, *First-Time Adoption of International Financial Reporting Standards*, primarily to allow an entity, at its date of transition to IFRS in its separate financial statements, to use a deemed cost to account for an investment in a subsidiary, jointly controlled entity or associate. An entity would be permitted to choose as deemed cost of such investments either their fair value or the previous GAAP carrying amount at the date of transition.

## ¶ 3816. Group Cash-Settled Share-Based Payment Arrangements (proposed IFRS)

The proposed standard would amend IFRS 2, *Share-Based Payment*, to clarify that IFRS 2 applies to group accounting for goods or services received from a supplier (including employees) when the supplier will receive cash payments linked to the price of the entity's equity instruments or to the price of the parent's equity instruments.

## ¶ 3817. Changes in Contributions to Employee Share Purchase Plans (draft IFRIC Interpretation)

IFRIC has reached the following tentative consensuses:

- If an employee, while remaining in the entity's employment, ceases to contribute to an employee share purchase plan (ESPP) and, as a consequence, is no longer able to buy shares under the plan, the event would be accounted for as a cancellation under IFRS 2, *Share-based Payment* (i.e., the amount that otherwise would have been recognized for services received over the remainder of the vesting period would be recognized immediately).

- If an employee changes from one ESPP to another, the event would be accounted for as a modification of the original grant, if the equity instruments granted to the employee under the new ESPP are deemed replacements for the equity instruments granted under the original ESPP; otherwise it would be accounted for as a cancellation, with participation in the new ESPP deemed a new grant of equity instruments.

## ¶ 3818. Multi-Employer Defined Benefit Plans (draft IFRIC Interpretation)

IFRIC has reached the following draft consensuses:

- To meet the definition of a multi-employer plan, the contribution and benefit levels would have to be determined without regard to the identity of the employer-entity that employs the employees concerned (i.e., there is some sharing between the participants in the plan of the actuarial risks associated with their current and former employees); thus, participation in a multi-employer plan would create different assets and liabilities for the participating employers from those that would arise for such employers if they had single entity plans.

- To apply defined benefit accounting to a multi-employer plan it would be necessary to measure the liabilities in the plan on the basis of assumptions that apply to the plan as a whole (i.e., not of a specific entity); plan assets would be measured at fair value and the assumptions required for the expected return on assets would apply to the plan as a whole.

- A determination would have to be made regarding whether there is a consistent and reliable basis of allocation of the plan across the participants.

- Amounts allocated to the entity for the components of defined benefit cost would be recognized in accordance with the requirements of IAS 19, *Em-*

*ployee Benefits*; note, however, that if enough information is not available to apply defined benefit accounting, an otherwise defined benefit multi-employer plan would be accounted for as a defined contribution plan.

## ¶ 3819. Hedges of a Net Investment in a Foreign Operation (draft IFRIC Interpretation)

The draft Interpretation addresses various issues related to an investment in a foreign operation held directly by a parent or indirectly through one or more subsidiaries. IFRIC has reached the following tentative consensuses:

- In a hedge of the foreign currency risks arising from a net investment in a foreign operation, the hedged item could be an amount of net assets equal to or less than the carrying amount of the net assets of the foreign operation in the consolidated financial statements of the parent entity.

- The hedged risk could be designated as the foreign currency exposure arising between the functional currency of the foreign operation and the functional currency of any parent entity (i.e., the immediate, intermediate, or ultimate parent entity of that foreign operation).

- Hedge accounting could not be applied to the foreign exchange differences arising between the functional currency of the foreign operation and the presentation currency of the parent entity.

- A derivative or a non-derivative instrument (or a combination thereof) could be used as a hedging instrument in a hedge of a net investment in a foreign operation and which could be held by any entity within the group (except the foreign operation that itself is being hedged), as long as the designation, documentation, and effectiveness requirements of IAS 39, *Financial Instruments: Recognition and Measurement*, are satisfied.

- For the purpose of assessing effectiveness, the change in value of the hedging instrument in respect of foreign exchange risk would be computed by reference to the functional currency of the parent entity against whose functional currency the hedged risk is measured in accordance with the hedge accounting documentation; depending on where the hedging instrument is held, the total change in value would be recorded in profit or loss, or equity, or both.

- An exposure to foreign currency risk arising from a net investment in a foreign operation could qualify for hedge accounting only once; thus, if the same risk is hedged by more than one parent entity within the group (e.g., a direct and an indirect parent entity), only one hedge relationship would qualify for hedge accounting in the consolidated financial statements.

## ¶ 3820. Real Estate Sales (draft IFRIC Interpretation)

The draft Interpretation would clarify whether sale agreements entered into before construction is complete should be regarded as construction contracts within the scope of IAS 11, *Construction Contracts*, or as agreements for the sale of goods within the scope of IAS 18, *Revenue*; in addition, it would provide revised guidance on the application of IAS 18 to real estate sales in general.

IFRIC has reached the following tentative consensuses:

- IAS 11 would apply if the sale agreement meets the definition of a construction contract in IAS 11; IAS 18 would apply if the sale agreement is instead an agreement for the sale of goods (i.e., completed real estate).

- If a sale agreement is for the sale of goods, revenue would be recognized when all the conditions for a sale in IAS 18 have been satisfied.

- In assessing whether all the risks and rewards of ownership and effective control over the goods have been transferred to the buyer, the assessment should be made in respect of the underlying real estate in its current state, rather than to the buyer's right to acquire the fully constructed real estate at a later date.

- If the real estate is sold with a degree of continuing involvement by the seller that effective control and the risks and rewards of ownership are not transferred when the buyer obtains possession, the nature and extent of the seller's continuing involvement would determine how the transaction is accounted for; if it is accounted for as a sale, the continuing involvement of the seller could delay the recognition of revenue.

- If the conditions in IAS 18 for recognizing revenue from the sale of the real estate are satisfied before the entity has performed all of its contractual obligations to the buyer, the seller's remaining obligations would be accounted for as follows:

  —To the extent that the seller has to perform further work on the real estate already delivered to the buyer (e.g., to remedy minor defects or complete internal decoration), an expense would be recognized.

  —To the extent that the seller has to deliver further goods or services that are separately identifiable from the real estate already delivered to the buyer, the remaining goods or services would be treated as a separate component of the sale; the fair value of the total consideration received and receivable from the buyer would be allocated between the components already delivered and those not yet delivered. Consideration allocated to the goods or services not yet delivered would be recognized as revenue only when the applicable revenue recognition conditions have been met for such goods or services.

## ¶ 3821. Distribution of Non-Cash Assets to Owners (draft IFRIC Interpretation)

The draft Interpretation addresses the topic of accounting for a distribution of non-cash assets to owners in the form of a dividend. It would require that the dividend payable be measured at the fair value of the assets to be distributed. If owners are given a choice of receiving either cash or a non-cash asset, measurement of the liability would have to take account of (1) the fair value of each alternative, and (2) the associated probability of which choice the owners would make. At each reporting date, the carrying amount of the dividend payable would be adjusted together with a corresponding increase or decrease to the amount of the distribution. Upon settlement of the dividend liability, any difference between the carrying amount of the assets distributed and the carrying amount of the dividend payable would be recognized in profit or loss.

## ¶ 3822. Contributions Received from Customers (draft IFRIC Interpretation)

The draft Interpretation addresses the issue of accounting for (1) contributions of property, plant, and equipment from customers (or others) that require the entity (referred to as the access provider) to provide access to a supply of goods or services to such customers, or (2) contributions of cash from customers that must be used to acquire or construct items of property, plant, and equipment that provide such access. The Interpretation would require access providers to:

- Recognize the contributed resource as an asset (measured at fair value) if the entity controls the resource and expected future benefits from such resource will flow to the entity.

- Recognize as a corresponding liability the obligation to provide customers with access to a supply of goods or services (i.e., which may arise as a result of a contract or may be a constructive obligation based on the entity's past actions).

- Recognize revenue over the period during which the entity has an obligation to provide access using the contributed asset (but which may not exceed the useful economic life of the related asset).

In respect of a cash contribution, if the item of property, plant, and equipment that must be acquired or constructed does not meet the definition of an asset, such cash would be accounted for as proceeds received in advance toward providing the asset to the customer.

# ¶ 3900. Interoffice Memoranda

## ¶ 3901. Inter-office Memo for Audit Professional of Public Accounting Firm

**To:** All Audit Partners and Staff

**From:** National Director of SEC Practice

**Subject:** Response to New SEC Rules Allowing Foreign Issuers to File IFRS Statements without Reconciliations to U.S. GAAP

The SEC, in Release No. 33-8879, recently adopted new rules permitting foreign companies registered with the Commission to file financial statements prepared in conformity with International Financial Reporting Standards (IFRS) without also having to provide reconciliations of reported net income and stockholders' equity to corresponding amounts under U.S. GAAP. The new rules are effective for calendar year 2008 financial statements.

Summary of the New Rules

Any foreign private issuer filing on Form 20-F is allowed to omit the required reconciliations to U.S. GAAP, whether the issuer complied with IFRS voluntarily or in accordance with the requirements of its home country regulator. The specific eligibility conditions are:

- Only IFRS *as issued by the IASB* may be applied.
- The issuer must state unreservedly and explicitly in a note to the financial statements that the statements are in compliance with IFRS as issued by the IASB (and, optionally, may also state that the financial statements are in accordance with its home country standards); the new rules do not apply to issuers filing financial statements based *solely* on a jurisdictional version or other variation of IFRS.
- The issuer's independent auditors must render an opinion concerning compliance with IFRS as issued by the IASB (and, optionally, may also render an opinion regarding compliance with standards required by the issuer's home country).

The Future of IFRS

The use of IFRS has, over recent years, become increasingly widespread throughout the world. Presently, approximately 100 countries now require or permit the application of IFRS, with other countries having incorporated them into their national standards, and still other countries planning to do so in the near term. All companies whose securities are listed on an EU regulated market that are incorporated in one of the 27 countries comprising the European Union *must* use IFRS as the basis of preparation for their consolidated statements. In addition, IFRS is required in the three European Economic Area countries of Iceland, Lichtenstein, and Norway, as well as in Australia and New Zealand. Canada and Israel are among the countries planning to adopt IFRS as their national standards in the future.

While the FASB and the IASB continue their efforts to converge the two sets of standards, variations exist now—and are expected to exist in the future. The SEC has also recently issued a concept release seeking comments regarding the possibility of providing U.S. domestic issuers with the option to prepare financial statements in conformity with either U.S. GAAP or IFRS. We expect that, in the near term (i.e., within the next year or two), the SEC, in support of efforts of the FASB and the IASB to create a universal set of high-quality, globally accepted standards to be used in cross-border financing, will, in fact, adopt rules under which U.S. public companies will also be able to use IFRS.

Even now, the following market forces are in play that provide our U.S. public clients with an impetus to adopt IFRS as a *parallel system* to U.S. GAAP in preparation for the future:

- As the number of non-U.S. companies reporting financial results in accordance with IFRS continues to increase, there is pressure on U.S. companies in many sectors and industries to prepare financial reports on the basis of IFRS to enable better comparisons among international companies and thus lead to a more efficient and effective allocation of capital by lenders and investors.

- As more countries accept IFRS financial statements for local regulatory or statutory filing purposes, subsidiaries of U.S. companies based in those jurisdictions will be preparing and filing their local financial statements using IFRS.

### Implications for the Firm

The new rules will create opportunities and challenges for the firm. We will be called upon to brief SEC clients on the main elements of IFRS standards and IFRIC interpretations and on the principal differences between IFRS and U.S. GAAP. It is also possible that foreign subsidiaries of our U.S. clients that use IFRS will no longer be submitting accompanying U.S. GAAP reconciliations to their U.S. parent companies; instead, the burden of conversion to U.S. GAAP for purposes of consolidation will be borne here. Without the benefit of those reconciliations (1) our knowledge of IFRS must be sharpened, and (2) our audit plans and procedures must be modified accordingly.

In addition, we must begin now to prepare for the inevitability that, even if it does not replace U.S. GAAP for our U.S. public clients, the role of IFRS in the United States and throughout the world will continue to grow.

## ¶ 3902. Inter-office Memo

**To:** All Members of the Corporate Financial Reporting and Compliance Staff

**From:** Chief Financial Officer

**Subject:** Response to New SEC Rules Allowing Foreign Issuers to File IFRS Statements without Reconciliations to U.S. GAAP

The SEC, in Release No. 33-8879, recently adopted new rules permitting foreign companies registered with the Commission to file financial statements prepared in conformity with International Financial Reporting Standards (IFRS) without also having to provide reconciliations of reported net income and stockholders' equity to corresponding amounts under U.S. GAAP. The new rules are effective for calendar year 2008 financial statements.

Summary of the New Rules

Any foreign private issuer filing on Form 20-F is allowed to omit the required reconciliations to U.S. GAAP, whether the issuer complied with IFRS voluntarily or in accordance with the requirements of its home country regulator. The specific eligibility conditions are:

- Only IFRS *as issued by the IASB* may be applied.

- The issuer must state unreservedly and explicitly in a note to the financial statements that the statements are in compliance with IFRS as issued by the IASB (and, optionally, may also state that the financial statements are in accordance with its home country standards); the new rules do not apply to issuers filing financial statements based *solely* on a jurisdictional version or other variation of IFRS.

- The issuer's independent auditors must render an opinion concerning compliance with IFRS as issued by the IASB (and, optionally, may also render an opinion regarding compliance with standards required by the issuer's home country).

The Future of IFRS

The use of IFRS has, over recent years, become increasingly widespread throughout the world. Presently, approximately 100 countries now require or permit the application of IFRS, with other countries having incorporated them into their national standards, and still other countries planning to do so in the near term. All companies whose securities are listed on an EU regulated market that are incorporated in one of the 27 countries comprising the European Union *must* use IFRS as the basis of preparation for their consolidated statements. In addition, IFRS is required in the three European Economic Area countries of Iceland, Lichtenstein, and Norway, as well as in Australia and New Zealand. Canada and Israel are among the countries planning to adopt IFRS as their national standards in the future.

While the FASB and the IASB continue their efforts to converge the two sets of standards, variations exist now—and are expected to exist in the future. The SEC has also recently issued a concept release seeking comments regarding the possibility of providing U.S. domestic issuers with the option to prepare financial statements in conformity with either U.S. GAAP or IFRS. We expect that, in the near term (i.e., within the next year or two), the SEC, in support of efforts of the FASB and the IASB to create a universal set of high-quality, globally accepted standards to be used in cross-border financing, will, in fact, adopt rules under which U.S. public companies will also be able to use IFRS.

Even now, the following market forces are in play that provide an impetus for our company to adopt IFRS as a *parallel system* to U.S. GAAP:

- As the number of non-U.S. companies reporting financial results in accordance with IFRS continues to increase, there is pressure on U.S. companies in many sectors and industries (including ours) to prepare financial reports on the basis of IFRS to enable better comparisons among international companies in our industry-thus leading to a more efficient and effective allocation of capital by lenders and investors and a lower cost of capital for our company.

- As more countries accept IFRS financial statements for local regulatory or statutory filing purposes, our subsidiaries based in those jurisdictions will be preparing and filing their local financial statements using IFRS.

Implications for the Company

We are investigating the possibility that our foreign subsidiaries will no longer be preparing and submitting U.S. GAAP reconciliations for consolidation purposes. Instead, the burden of conversion to U.S. GAAP will be handled at corporate.

Without the benefit of those reconciliations (1) our knowledge of IFRS must be sharpened, and (2) we must become familiar with the differences between IFRS and U.S. GAAP. We expect to call on our auditors to assist us in this regard.

In addition, we must begin now to prepare for the inevitability that, even if it does not replace U.S. GAAP for our U.S. public clients, we may choose to adopt IFRS as our primary basis of accounting in the near future.